The Political Philosophy
of James Madison

15.26

THE
POLITICAL PHILOSOPHY OF
James Madison

BY

GARRETT WARD SHELDON

The Johns Hopkins University Press
Baltimore & London

© 2001 The Johns Hopkins University Press
All rights reserved. Published 2001
Printed in the United States of America on acid-free paper

Johns Hopkins Paperbacks edition, 2002
2 4 6 8 9 7 5 3 1

The Johns Hopkins University Press
2715 North Charles Street
Baltimore, Maryland 21218-4363
www.press.jhu.edu

The Library of Congress has cataloged the hardcover edition of this book as follows:

Sheldon, Garrett Ward, 1954–
The political philosophy of James Madison / Garrett Ward Sheldon.
    p.   cm.
Includes bibliographical references and index.
ISBN 0-8018-6479-8 (hardcover)
1. Madison, James, 1751–1836 — Contributions in political science. I. Title.
JC211.M35 S44 2000
321.8′092 — dc21
00-008659

ISBN 0-8018-7106-9 (pbk.)

A catalog record for this book is available from the British Library.

FOR

the promise of Madison's republic

CONTENTS

PREFACE

AFTER THE PUBLICATION of *The Political Philosophy of Thomas Jefferson* (Baltimore: Johns Hopkins University Press, 1991), its reprinting in India (1993), and its translation into Russian and publication in Moscow (1996), several colleagues asked what research in Early American political thought I would next pursue. David Rouse, a philosophy professor at my college in Virginia, suggested James Madison. This seemed inspired to me. This book is the result of that colleague's suggestion. Whether that is an example of Hegel's "Cunning of Reason in History" or St. Augustine's notion of Providence, I leave to the reader.

I am grateful for the continuing counsel and encouragement of Carey McWilliams of Rutgers University, Rick Battistoni of Providence College, Daniel Dreisbach at American University, and David Eastwood of Pembroke College, Oxford.

Anita Rivera Simpkins' University of Virginia doctoral dissertation, "James Madison on Education" (May 1998), for which I served as an outside reader, greatly contributed to the chapter on Madison's own education.

The patience, forbearance, and encouragement of my editor at the Johns Hopkins University Press, Henry Y. K. Tom, has been truly a blessing and exemplary of the best in academic scholarship and publishing.

My family's understanding during many mornings of writing is greatly appreciated.

A summer research grant from the Faculty Development Committee of my college was very helpful. The endowed John Morton Beaty Professorship was very beneficial at this time.

Finally, Linda Meade's skillful preparation of the manuscript, especially her expertise on chasing down stubborn footnotes, and Celestia Ward's skillful copyediting are gratefully acknowledged.

INTRODUCTION

Liberalism, Classical Republicanism,
and Christianity in the Political
Philosophy of James Madison

BY THE END of the millennium, scholarship concerning early American political theory had reached a basic consensus, namely that three main ideologies existed during the Revolutionary and early Republican periods: Lockean liberalism, classical republicanism, and Protestant Christianity.[1]

This book examines the historical development of James Madison's political philosophy through the periods of colonial America, the American Revolution, and the establishment and early development of the American Republic, with reference to the classics of Western political theory (Aristotle, Locke, Montesquieu, etc.) and the contemporary historiographic scholarship that addresses the contrasting influences of liberalism, classical republicanism, and Christianity. Like my book on Jefferson, this study shows that the political ideas of this "father of the U.S. Constitution" developed and changed over time, given the exigencies of American social and political history, and drew upon a wide range of theoretical traditions. Also like the Jefferson study, this book reveals an underlying coherence throughout that development, possibly attributable to Madison's early education in Protestant Christianity. It reveals that Madison's shifts in emphasis between Lockean liberalism and classical republicanism (or centralized federalism and decentralized states' rights) are best understood in reference to the Calvinist culture and worldview that Madison had imbibed from his Scottish tutors and from Dr. John Witherspoon at Princeton. These influences provided a vision of human nature and political society as volatile and imperfect, always in need of balancing and moderation.

Madison expressed this perspective in several of his *Federalist Papers*, for example, when he wrote that "there is a degree of depravity in mankind which requires a certain degree of circumspection and distrust," commending a governmental system that is designed to pit "ambition against ambition," recognizing man's "imperfections and weaknesses" which historically have caused political "quarrels, jealousies, and envy" prompted by "love of preeminence" and "wounded pride."[2] As the *Westminster Confession*, the creedal authority of English Calvinism familiar to all colonial Presbyterians, put it, "From . . . original corruption . . . we are utterly indisposed, disabled, and made opposite to all good and wholly inclined to all evil."[3] Such "vindictiveness" leading to factions and oppression is "sown in the nature of man," according to Madison, and is the "experience of the ages."[4] Only a constitution that acknowledges this fallen nature of humanity and constructs "checks and balances" to ameliorate its negative consequences can hope to avoid political oppression of one sort or another.

In Madison's view, American federalism's balancing of local and states' rights classical republicanism (whose evil shows itself in the oppression of the minority rich by the majority poor, requiring Lockean protection of individual natural rights) with centralized national power (whose wicked tendency is the concentration of power and financial corruption, requiring decentralized democracy to control it) can best ensure the tempering of human nature's tendency to use politics to advance selfish interests. This American system, combined with the dividing of political authority in overlapping branches (executive, judicial, and legislative) in both state and national governments, would have the best chance of avoiding tyranny and oppression. Madison's Christian worldview, then, led to his faith in the American constitution's accurate assessment of human nature to prevent either democracy's tendency towards anarchy or the executive's tendency towards dictatorship.

Depending on where he saw the greatest threat to a balanced stability and individual liberty (decentralized classical republicanism or nationalist Lockean liberalism), Madison shifted his emphasis to the other cause and argued effectively for its importance to American liberty. His Calvinist appreciation of a political "calling" or public vocation from God also evinced Madison's reformed leanings. This extended even to the Puritan tendency to allow clergy to serve as magistrates. When Jefferson's draft constitution for Virginia prohibited ministers from serving in government, Madison responded: "Does not the exclusion of Ministers of the Gospel as such violate a fundamental principle of liberty by punishing a religious profession with the privation of a civil right?"[5] His arguments that religious liberty would ensure the purity of the Christian faith similarly show the influence of the *Westminster Confession*, which states: "God alone is the Lord of the conscience and has left it free from the doctrines and commandments of men."[6]

As a delegate to the Continental Congress during the American Revolution (1780–83), Madison experienced directly the difficulties of conducting a unified and effective war effort without sufficient central authority over the states. This lack of coordination under the Articles of Confederation during the Revolution was compounded by the social turmoil in several states after the war, leading Madison to fear that without a strong new national government, the American states would become subservient to the wars and politics of Europe. At the same time, the radically democratic policies of the majority of citizens in the newly independent states threatened to permit the violation of the Lockean natural rights to life, liberty, and property, for which the Revolution had been fought. Hence, Madison's early post-Revolutionary political thought, developed as a delegate to the Constitutional Convention and reflected in his contributions to the *Federalist Papers,* evince a Lockean liberal concern for individual natural rights, limited government, and economic freedom, to be preserved through an enlarged republic under a strong central regime, encouraging a diversity of interests that would counterbalance one another and preventing the oppression of minorities or individual rights by the majority or local community. It was Madison's fear over close "classical republican" democratic communities' potential for tyranny over minority and *individual* rights, along with the widely held Calvinist suspicion about the motives of sinful men, that led him to construct a constitution that provided for a strong central government with power over state laws to protect individual liberties and provide checks to "spiteful" human interests as well as selfish parochial prejudices.

However, after the ratification of the constitution and ascendance of the High Federalists to national power (notably during the administration of President John Adams), Madison perceived another threat to natural rights, this one emanating from human arrogance and greed, from a faction representing narrow financial interests and the "consolidation" of power in the central government to advance those interests. Growing from national leaders' pride and vanity, pomp and arrogance, the Alien and Sedition Acts insulated powerful men from criticism or correction, potentially allowing them to rule in perpetuity—potentially establishing, for Madison, a de facto monarchy. His response, with Jefferson, in the Virginia and Kentucky Resolutions (1798–99), invoked classical republican arguments in favor of states' rights for protecting civil liberties (especially those of free speech and freedom of the press against the Alien and Sedition Acts). Similarly, during Madison's two presidential terms (1809–17), his political philosophy was characterized first by a classical republican concern for ensuring frugal, virtuous government through an adherence to strictly enumerated congressional powers and repudiation of corrupting fiscal policies (the bank, government support of manufacturers, public improvement projects, etc.), and later it was characterized by an easing of restrictions on national power when beneficial to the national interest and safely contained by a Republican Congress. In other words, Madison's political philosophy historically shifted between Lockean liberal and classical republican, federalist and states' rights perspectives, with a consistent view to a balanced, moderate government that accurately reflected the Christian view of human nature as egotistical and domineering, realistically establishing a stable and just regime. The threads of Lockean, classical, and reformed Christian ideas were thus woven together in Madison's political thought.

Even later in his life, when advising on political affairs from his retirement at the estate at Montpelier, Madison saw as the greatest threat to the American system the states' rights nullification policies of South Carolina's John C. Calhoun. So his final political writings, like those of the earlier *Federalist* period, focused on the preservation of the Union as necessary to avoid anarchy, chaos, and ultimately, tyranny. His posthumously published "Advice to My Country" revealed this concern, alluding to the danger as "the Serpent creeping with his deadly wiles into Paradise."[7]

Madison's movement between Lockean and classical philosophical perspectives was also often guided by the Christian realist view of man's weak, sinful nature—people are prone to pride, arrogance, and the oppressive use of power for selfish ends (often masked in deceptively virtuous rhetoric), requiring institutional checks and balances to prevent such evils and violence. When those dangers came from local community egalitarianism, the remedy was nationally protected individual rights to property, religion, and so on; when the principal threat was from centralized power and its temptations towards tyranny, the proper check was from localized state democracies. American constitutionalism addresses the underlying cause of political strife with a structure inhibiting any individual's or group's inordinate power. That view of human nature upon which Madison constructed the American constitutional system reflects a reformed Christian education common throughout the Colonies, one that regarded humankind as inevitably imperfect—ever plagued by sinful desires for power and domination over others. Therefore, all earthly regimes are inherently potential tools for oppression unless structured in such a way as to pit "ambition against ambition" through competing levels and branches of government.

While most studies of Madison make reference to his Calvinist education, few fully develop the implications of this Augustinian theology for his political philosophy.[8] Merrill Peterson, in *James Madison: A Biography in His Own Words*, notes that Princeton was the "academic citadel of Presbyterianism in the New World" when Madison studied there (1769–72) and that he remained there for six months after graduation to study Hebrew and theology with Dr. Witherspoon, but Peterson does not present the components of that doctrine which Madison imbues at a crucial stage of his intellectual development or their significance to his political theory.

Yet Madison's writings are riddled with direct references and allusions to his religious background and its application to politics. In a letter to a college friend shortly after this period, Madison declares that the truest testimony of religious conviction lies in prominent men declaring their "fervent Advocacy in the cause of Christ." His energetic efforts in disestablishing the Anglican Church in Virginia soon thereafter flowed from an avowed attempt to abolish the "ignorance and corruption" of the state-supported church and end the "diabolical Hell" of the political persecution of Christian orthodoxy suffered by Presbyterian and Baptist churches. Believing that "religious bondage debilitates the mind and unfits it for noble enterprises," Madison argued that the legal "inquisition" of Anglican Virginia distorted the proper Christian "means of salvation" through "example and forbearance."[9] So, ultimately, James Madison's political vision relies on the separation of church and state, with the former educating citizens in their moral duties and the latter restraining them from their worst excesses. The Augustinian and reformed Christian essence of this view of the "best" regime and its use of both Lockean and classical political philosophy has not been adequately presented; this motivates the discussion of James Madison's political philosophy found herein.[10]

There is considerable evidence that James Madison adhered to this Christian perspective early in his life (having imbued it through his education at Princeton) and late in his life (after retiring from the presidency); but there is less explicit testimony to traditional Christianity, except conceptually, during his long career in public service. As a young man he may have been an advocate of "the cause of Christ," and as an elderly man he called the Christian faith "the best and purest religion," which is "so essential to the moral order of the World and to the happiness of man, that arguments which enforce it cannot be drawn from too many sources"; but during his years in governmental service Madison never explicitly mentions his personal beliefs.[11] He may have become more reticent about explicitly expressing his faith because religion had already become a divisive issue in American society after the revolution, just when Madison was trying to forge national unity through the new constitution.[12] Several scholars have linked American theology to this founder's political thought, but this study may help to explain Madison's shifts between modern liberalism and classical republicanism during his long and thoughtful public service.[13]

CHAPTER ONE

INTELLECTUAL HERITAGE

Politics, Philosophy, and Theology

*The principles and Modes of Government are too important
to be disregarded by an Inquisitive Mind and I think are
well worthy a critical examination by all students that have
health and leisure.*

—James Madison, 1773

JAMES MADISON is often referred to as the "Father of the Constitution." There are several reasons for this. He was one of the most active and constructive of the delegates to the Constitutional Convocation in Philadelphia in 1787 (after having early on advocated reform of the Articles of Confederation); he contributed substantially to the Convention compromises that formed unanimity among the highly diverse colonies (while writing the most detailed record of the Constitutional Convocation's proceedings); and he was a prolific advocate for ratification of the document in his *Federalist Papers* and in private correspondence. Madison reduced the 189 complex proposed amendments to a simple 9 amendments, which eventually formed the Bill of Rights, themselves integral to the eventual ratification of the U.S. Constitution and integral to its ultimate political principles. He was also the leading advocate for constitutional ratification in the crucial Virginia convention. As such, Madison clearly deserves designation as a leading founder of the system of American constitutional government. As Lance Banning recently wrote, "James Madison did more to shape the early nation's com-

1

prehension of its governmental institutions than any other member of his generation."[1]

James Madison's pivotal role in the establishment of representative democracy in the United States of America grew from his intellectual leadership. One of his earliest writings, written when he was perhaps eight years old, was a poem copied from a British magazine into a notebook, referring to Virgil, Cicero, and Pope, and containing numerous citations to the Bible.[2] His writings and speeches evince a scholarly temper more marked than that of any other Founding Father. His was a learned, rigorous mind producing tightly reasoned, persuasively argued texts. Without the poetic flourishes of a Jefferson or the worldly wisdom of a Franklin, Madison's writings reflect the strict, ordered rationality characteristic of eighteenth-century Calvinist training: carefully reasoned, tightly constructed arguments familiar to the Presbyterian clerics who founded Princeton University, modeled on the clarity and rigor of John Calvin's *Institutes of the Christian Religion;* the same intellectual rigor that established Harvard as the Puritan citadel in New England. Madison displayed a cerebral, intellectual Christianity that did not divorce reason from faith but saw the two working together in complementarity for the greater glory of God; he had a reasoned and disciplined appreciation of Christ earlier associated with St. Augustine and the Catholic Jesuits.

Madison's naturally studious inclinations meshed nicely with this reformed Christian emphasis on a learned faith. John Marshall once remarked that if eloquence included the unadorned power of reasonable persuasion, Madison was "the most eloquent man I ever heard."[3] William Pierce, a Georgia delegate to the Constitutional Convention, said that "every person seems to acknowledge his greatness. He blends together the profound politician with the Scholar." Pierce found in Madison "a most agreeable, eloquent and convincing speaker" who was always "the best informed man of any point in debate" at the Constitutional Convention, where "in the management of every great question he evidently took the lead." In private, Pierce found Madison displaying "a most agreeable style of conversation" with "a remarkably sweet temper" and "great modesty."[4] Thomas Jefferson, no mean intellectual himself, remarked on the "rich and ready resources" of the "luminous and discriminating mind" of his lifelong friend and colleague.[5] Madison's training at Princeton, which Merrill Peterson calls "the academic citadel of Presbyterianism" in eighteenth-century America, marked him intellectually for life. His thoughtful religious faith, reverence for Scripture, and view of his political career as a divine "calling" all reveal these Princeton roots. A lifetime of rational discourse, respect for knowledge, and intellectual honesty ended with his dying words to his niece that his death was "Nothing more than a change of mind, my dear."

Yet Madison's character was also always known for its ready, if wry, sense of humor. Friends and acquaintances often reported his stock of amusing stories and easy laughter. During the U.S. Constitution ratifying Convention in Virginia, Madison worked with a fellow federalist delegate named George Nicholas, who was famous for his grotesque obesity. When someone showed Madison a caricature of Nicholas "as a plum pudding with legs on it," Madison reportedly laughed until tears came to his eyes.[6]

Madison's early education began at home. Because of his mother's frail, often infirm condition and his father's frequent occupation managing a busy plantation, young "Jemmy's" earliest education was relegated to his paternal grandmother, Frances Taylor Madison. Remembered as a pious Christian woman (she had provided the local Anglican church with part of its communion plate), she was also a learned one, drawing on her son's eighty-five-volume personal library for James's education.[7] Not a robust boy and frequently confined to a sickbed like his mother, young Madison formed studious habits while confined at home, developing an early love of scholarly investigation and contemplation. When healthy, Madison enjoyed walking and riding amid the natural beauty of the Virginia mountains, observing the profuse wildlife and flora.

His family was typical of the early Virginia settlers — commencing as tradesmen and growing into landed gentry.[8] His great-grandfather James Taylor II explored the region around central Virginia's Blue Ridge Mountains in 1716 as part of the royal governor's land-surveying expedition. Taylor received 13,500 acres near the Rapidan River, a patrimony in Orange County that descended to his daughter, Frances Taylor, who married Ambrose Madison, the son of a ship's carpenter who had settled in Virginia in the mid-seventeenth century. The son of Ambrose and Frances Madison, James Sr., settled an estate of 4,000 acres in Piedmont, Virginia, and with his wife, nee Nelly Conway, raised twelve children, James Madison Jr. being the first. So Madison grew up in a rural setting among a large family of brothers and sisters and numerous neighboring kin. He was baptized in the established Church of England—a local parish in which his father served as vestryman.[9] Douglas Adair notes in his introduction of James Madison's autobiography, "Madison's memoir gives striking proof that his whole life, by deliberate choice, was lived in an atmosphere of books and study."[10]

Madison's education followed the typical routine of this eighteenth-century Virginia gentry: earliest education taking place in the family, followed by private tutoring either at home or in a nearby boarding school (invariably by a clergyman), and then finally college, either in the colonies(William and Mary College, Princeton, Yale, or Harvard) or in the mother country of England (Oxford or Cambridge). When Madison was eleven or twelve years old, his grandmother sent away to London for an eight-volume collection of England's famous literary magazine, the *Spectator,* edited by Joseph Addison. This periodical, which Madison later praised for its examples of "fine writing," contained intelligent essays, often satirical, about contemporary figures and ideas, emphasizing education, morals, and the reform of manners. It claimed to advance "truth, innocence, honor and virtue, as the chief ornaments of life." Madison later told one of his nephews that he found Addison "of the first rank among the fine writers of the age." Reading such good literature, he later said, would improve one's own writing "for the benefit of others, and for your own reputation."[11]

At the age of twelve, Madison was sent to a boarding school in King and Queen County, seventy miles from his home. The Reverend Donald Robertson, a Scottish minister educated at Aberdeen and the University of Edinburgh (the heart of Scottish Calvinism), taught Madison Latin, Greek, French, mathematics, geography, literature, and theology. Madison later described his "middle school" teacher as "a man of extensive learning, and a distinguished teacher."[12] For five years he learned under this Presbyterian minister (later saying "all that I have been in life I owe largely to that man"), keeping notebooks on his studies of John Locke, Plato,

Fontenelle, and Euclid. Most of his lessons were couched in Christian religious terms, such as the logical syllogism Madison recorded in a notebook:

1. No sinners are happy.
2. Angels are happy; therefore
3. Angels are not sinners.[13]

Directed by Reverend Robertson, Madison probably also read Justinian's *Institute,* Montesquieu's *Spirit of the Laws,* Thomas à Kempis's *Imitation of Christ,* and the "Bible" of English Calvinism, the *Westminster Confession.*[14] It was probably at Robertson's school that Madison took notes on the *Memoirs* of Cardinal de Retz (a favorite of Calvinists for his tolerance of French Huguenots and political realism), including the epigram "Except Religion and Good Manners everything else is indifferent."[15] The *Madison Papers'* editors found that Robertson's account book contains a list of books in his library. The list clearly indicates that:

> Under Robertson's tutelage, JM could have taken the notes on Montaigne's *Essays* and, incidentally, have gained his initial acquaintance with Montesquieu's *The Spirit of the Laws* and Locke's *An Essay Concerning Human Understanding.* Moreover, he studied there almost all the Latin classics from which he quotes in his notebook, as well as others he found no occasion to cite. The "Account Book" reveals "Jamie" Madison buying works by Virgil, Horace, Justinian, and Cornelius Nepos, and probably also reading others by Caesar, Tacitus, Lucretius, Eutropius, and Phaedrus. With Robertson as his mentor, JM used selections from the writings of Plutarch, Herodotus, Thucydides, and Plato in his study of Greek. Abel Boyer's *The Compleat French Master for Ladies and Gentlemen* may have introduced JM to the French language.[16]

The Reverend Robertson showed he connected his faith with practical matters when he wrote in his account bank after Madison's last tuition payment, "Deo Gratia and Gloria" ("Thanks and glory be to God").[17]

At sixteen, Madison moved back home to continue his education with the Reverend Thomas Martin, the new pastor of his parents'

local parish church. A Scottish-Irish minister recently graduated
from the "evangelical Calvinist" College of New Jersey (Princeton),
the twenty-five-year-old Martin inspired Madison to study at this
Calvinist Christian institution rather than at the "decadent" Anglican college in Williamsburg, Virginia. From Princeton Madison
wrote to the Reverend Martin: "Your kind advice and friendly cau-
tions are a favor that shall always be gratefully remembered."[18] The
reputation for lax morality and an unhealthy climate at the College
of William and Mary may also have influenced James Madison Sr.'s
decision to send his eldest son north to college. While the older
Virginia institution was in decline and tainted by association with
royalist, Anglican ideology, Princeton was perceived as an up-and-
coming institution, the "academic citadel of Presbyterianism in the
New World," led by a dynamic new president, Scotsman Dr. John
Witherspoon, and emanating both religious revival and rampant
republicanism.[19] Its evangelical Calvinism contrasted with the dry,
cold, formal ritualism and weak Arminianism of the Anglican atmosphere in Williamsburg. Brant referred to it as a large "Scotch
boarding school." An Episcopal bishop who later knew Madison
summarized this decision by saying that "Mr. Madison was sent to
Princeton College—perhaps through fear of the skeptical principles
then so prevalent at William and Mary. During his stay at Princeton
a great revival took place, and it was believed that he partook of its
spirit. On his return home he conducted worship in his father's
house."[20]

PRINCETON

Princeton University (originally called the College of New Jersey)
was founded during the Great Awakening—a series of Christian revivals in the colonies lasting from the 1730s to the 1770s. Associated
with the Anglican evangelist George Whitefield and Puritan divine
Jonathan Edwards, these Christian revivals spread across the American colonies, producing widespread dramatic conversions (often
accompanied by emotional displays of weeping and shouting at
large outdoor preaching services), sincere repentance, and reformed
lives and morals.[21] Emphasizing the spiritual New Birth that Jesus
told Nicodemus was necessary to enter the Kingdom of Heaven

(John 3:5–8), this move of the Holy Spirit across America, like that in the Biblical account of Pentecost (Acts 2:3–13), upset many staid religious leaders who preferred a highly ordered, rational worship and experience. Most church denominations split over the effects of the Great Awakening revivals: conservative "Old Lights" like Harvard College rejected the evangelical "enthusiasm" and emotion of this move of the Spirit (and eventually rejected the Spirit of Christ altogether by becoming predominantly Unitarian, highly intellectual, and sophisticated); lively "New Lights" welcomed the conviction of sin, sincere repentance, comfort of the Holy Spirit, and the personal commitment to Christ in everyday living that this revival spawned. The Middle Atlantic Scottish Presbyterians who favored this lively Christianity were called "New Side" Presbyterians. They established Princeton in the wilderness of central New Jersey, as a center of this Light of Christ, to preserve, as Reverend Jonathan Edwards put it, "the sweet spirit" of this vital Christianity and to train young ministers to carry it forward.[22]

The evangelistic New Lights emphasized the necessity of vital, or "experimental" religion; and they held that a divine call or "regenerating change" was more important in a ministerial candidate than strictly formal training.[23] In President John Witherspoon, the college obtained a scholarly New Light enthusiast. The spirit of religious liberty, in lively worship and grateful acceptance of the gifts of the Holy Spirit, later meshed nicely with the political liberty espoused by the American Revolutionary leaders, many of whom came out of Princeton. As Mark Noll writes, "At Princeton . . . religious considerations were always central to the outworking of republican theory." At this college, professors spoke privately with their students about their spiritual development, met to pray together twice a day, lectured continually on the faith, encouraged informed student devotions, and prayed for revival. By the time Madison arrived at Princeton in 1769, under the presidency of Dr. Witherspoon, the college was training as many students for public service, business, and law as for the ministry of the gospel; but in the Calvinist fashion, these "secular" vocations were viewed as divine "callings" themselves, properly conducted for the glory of God and under Christ's guidance.[24] Worldly service, especially in government, was just another Christian vocation. While at Princeton, Madison noted in his extracts from William Burkitt's *Expository Notes, with Practical Observations on the New Testament of Our Lord and Savior Jesus Christ* that "Magistrates are not to be treated with ill words. . . . Titles of civil Honour and Respect given to persons in place and power are agreeable to the Mind and Will of God" (Acts 23:25; 25:25). And from the Proverbs of Solomon, he noted that "not all our religion that's [sic] in our brains and tongue, and nothing in our heart and life," for "it is not the *talking*, but the *walking* and *working* person that is the true Christian."[25]

Eighteen-year-old Madison traveled the 300 miles from Virginia to Princeton with his tutor Reverend Martin and immediately "tested out" of the first two years of college, passing freshman exams in English, Latin, Greek, mathematics, and New Testament Bible. He went on to finish the entire college course load in two years and stayed on for six more months of "graduate study" with Dr. Witherspoon (in Hebrew and theology—suggesting he was considering a career as a minister). Ironically, throughout his life, James Madison did look like a reformed minister, always wearing clergymen's black breeches and coat, as shown in the famous portrait by Thomas Sully.[26] At Princeton, Madison joined and probably helped found the American Whig Society; at the time, *Whig* meant "a Scotch Presbyterian or a Dissenting American Presbyterian." In the spirit of this Puritan theology, Madison wrote a poem for a student publication attacking decadent clergy, advising them to don no more "the garb of Christian wear."[27] Shortly after graduating from Princeton, Madison wrote to his college friend "Billy" Bradford that "there could not be a stronger testimony in favor of Religion . . . than for men who occupy the most honorable and gainful departments and are rising in reputation and wealth, publicly to declare their unsatisfactoriness by becoming fervent Advocates in the cause of Christ."[28]

The Princeton that Madison attended was entirely housed in the original stone building, Nassau Hall, now used for university administrators' offices. In old Nassau, student dormitories, classrooms, dining hall, library, and chapel combined to serve one hundred students and a dozen faculty. Every day at 5 A.M., the morning bell rang, awakening the college for 6 A.M. chapel services. An hour of study followed, after which students had breakfast, went to 9 o'clock recitation, studied until 1 o'clock, and had dinner. Afterward there was more recitation and study, 5 o'clock prayers, supper at 7 o'clock, and bed at 9 o'clock.[29] A regimen, I'm sure, similar to that conducted by Princeton students today. As one scholar summarized it:

> The education that James Madison and his friends received at the College of New Jersey stimulated deep thinking . . . and encouraged—but never demanded—a personal commitment of the student to Jesus Christ as Savior and Lord . . . the curriculum was not narrow, but was taught from the Christian perspective which meant that learning was developed within a framework of absolutes . . . the Sovereignty of God . . . His providence . . . the sinful nature of man which needs salvation, yet the great possibilities for good that man possesses when he is guided by His maker.[30]

During that time, beginning in 1770, Madison began taking "Notes on the Commentary on the Bible." Much of his Bible notes are exact quotations from Burkitt's *Expository Notes*, printed in 1724. They also contain passages from Acts 19–28; Proverbs 9–16, 18, and 20; Matthew 1–13, and 21; Luke 2; and John. Some of Madison's Bible notes have been lost, but their references, along with Madison's annotations, have been preserved by his first biographer, William Cabell Rives. He notes that Madison refers

> to a chapter of the Acts of the Apostles, where the Bereans are mentioned as "more noble than those in Thessalonica, in that they received the word with all readiness of mind, and searched the Scriptures daily whether these things were so," he commends their conduct "as a noble example for all succeeding Christians to imitate and follow."
>
> In a paraphrase on the Gospel of St. John, referring to the passage in which Mary Magdalene is represented as looking into the Holy Sepulchre and seeing two angels in white, one sitting at the head and the other at the feet, where the body of the Saviour had lain, he makes the following reflection, "Angels to be desired at our feet as well as at our head—not an angelical understanding and a diabolical conversation—not all our reli-

gion in our brains and tongue, and nothing in our heart and life."

In the same spirit, commenting on the chapter of Acts, where Jesus says to St. Paul, who had fallen to the earth under the light which shined round about him from heaven, "*Arise, and go* into the city, and it shall be told thee what thou shalt *do,*" he [Madison] subjoins this as the proper deduction from the passage: "It is not the *talking,* but the *walking* and *working* person that is the true Christian."[31]

Fifteen years after he left his studies at Princeton, and after much service to the cause of liberty it encouraged, Princeton bestowed the degree of doctor of laws on Madison in 1787, shortly after the constitution had been written.

TEACHER WITHERSPOON

A sense of the education that Madison received at Princeton can be gleaned from his notebooks and letters (with references to readings in Locke, Montesquieu, the Bible, Montaigne, and Socrates) and also from the records of lectures he received from President John Witherspoon, especially those on moral philosophy, which combined theology, politics, economics, and law. Witherspoon's lectures reveal a synthesis of the dominant ideologies of revolutionary America: Lockean liberalism, classical Republicanism, and Christian theology.[32] Witherspoon has been credited with influencing at Princeton one president (James Madison), one vice-president (Aaron Burr), ten cabinet officers, sixty members of Congress, twelve state governors, fifty-six state legislators, and thirty judges, including three justices of the Supreme Court.

John Adams met Dr. Witherspoon at Princeton while en route to Philadelphia in 1774 for the First Continental Congress. "He is as high a Son of Liberty, as any man in America," Adams declared of the native of Scotland.[33] Witherspoon confirmed that assessment two years later by being one of the fifty-six signers of the Declaration of Independence. For six years during the American Revolutionary War, Witherspoon served with distinction as a member of the Continental Congress, working closely with Madison during this formative time of the American Republic.

Still, throughout his long academic career and periods of political activism, he remained first a cleric, a staunch Scottish Presbyterian Calvinist minister steeped in the Scriptures, subscribing to the doctrines of the reformed Christian faith as spelled out in the *Westminster Confession* and viewing the world through a Protestant perspective—mindful of man's sinful nature, his redemption through God's grace and faith in Christ, and the continuing presence of evil in the world. Witherspoon was born into a clerical family on both sides: his father, James, a Presbyterian minister in Yester, Scotland, his mother, Anne, the daughter of the minister of Temple Parish in Edinburgh. His classical education ended at the University of Edinburgh, where he took a degree in divinity. The Reverend Witherspoon served in several churches in Scotland before accepting the invitation to become president of Princeton. His biographer Jack Scott notes that "At the conclusion of his studies in 1743, Witherspoon's theological views were formed; they remained essentially the same throughout his life."[34] These were Calvinist—with an Augustinian emphasis on original sin and salvation solely through God's grace, depraved sinful man being unable to do any good deed to merit God's favor "lest any man boast" (Eph. 2:8–9). The faith in that grace and in Jesus Christ's atonement for our sins, which granted us forgiveness from a loving God, commended a grateful humility and "realistic" appraisal of man's ability for (very limited) good. "There can be no true religion till there be a discovery of your lost state by nature and practice and an unfeigned acceptance of Christ Jesus as he is offered in the gospel," Witherspoon wrote. Scott insists that "in no other country had Calvinism taken deeper root or more profoundly affected national life than in Scotland. Witherspoon was of this tough and gnarled Scottish stock."[35]

In the doctrinal controversies of the eighteenth-century Scottish church, Witherspoon always sided with (and often led) the conservative and orthodox wing against the liberal movements that would water down this tough-minded faith with popular worldly philosophy or soft, humanist tendencies. Against what he termed "paganized Christian divines," Witherspoon led the evangelical charge with reliance on the Bible, fervent preaching of the Word on such topics as "All Mankind by Nature under Sin" and "Christ's Death a Proper Atonement for Sin," and adherence to Christian fundamentals. Mocking his liberal church opponents, Witherspoon once wrote that, for them, "all ecclesiastical persons . . . suspected of heresy, are to be esteemed men of great genius, vast learning, and uncommon worth; their authorities [in preaching sermons] must be drawn from heathen writers . . . as few as possible from Scripture." The reliance on non-Christian philosophy and psychology that eventually came to dominate the liberal American "mainline" denominations was rejected by Witherspoon during its earliest outbreak. He insisted on a Christianity firmly rooted in the Bible, in a Scripture revered as divinely inspired truth. From this basis of Christian orthodoxy on the nature of fallen man, on Jesus' divinity and God's providence and grace, Witherspoon believed all topics of knowledge could be safely investigated. So he was not opposed to the "liberal arts" curriculum at Princeton—the studies of philosophy, politics, nature and art—as long as they were viewed through the primacy of Christian truth.[36] Madison's lively intellect seems to have flourished in this atmosphere (it has been noted that he wrote commentaries on Scripture, while Jefferson edited Scripture to suit his tastes).

Dr. Witherspoon arrived in America in 1768, at the age of forty-five, to become the president of Princeton, just one year before Madison arrived there as a student. He came from Scotland with his wife, Elizabeth, and their five children. Nassau Hall was brilliantly illuminated with candles to welcome them, although the college was in such financial straits that it could not pay his entire ship passage. President Witherspoon immediately began a fund-raising campaign, preaching in churches all over America, and brought the Princeton ledger from red to black in two years.[37] He went on to enjoy a distinguished thirty-year career of academic leadership, James Madison being only one of many prominent graduates of Princeton. At the age of sixty-six, Witherspoon lost his beloved wife of forty-two years. Two years later, he shocked the staid Presbyterians of Princeton by marrying a twenty-four-year-old widow. While totally blind and living in retirement on his farm, he had two children by this second wife. He died in 1794, aged 71, the Biblical span of a man's natural life (Ps. 90:10).

The evidence for Dr. Witherspoon's influence on James Madison is both historical and conceptual. Madison referred to him with affection and respect as the "old Doctor" and defended Witherspoon's writings against the "peevish snarling" of his critics.[38] Besides studying closely with Witherspoon at Princeton, Madison served with him in the Continental Congress (1781–82) and frequently visited him during his trips from Philadelphia through New Jersey.[39] Witherspoon spoke glowingly of his brilliant student, telling Thomas Jefferson that "during the whole time [Madison] was under [my] tuition [I] never knew him to do, or say, an improper thing." Undoubtedly, President Witherspoon was involved in the decision to have Princeton award Madison an honorary Doctor of Laws degree shortly after the completion of the U.S. Constitution. At the ceremony conferring that degree, Witherspoon stated that "all concerned in this college were, not barely willing, but proud . . . [to honor] one of their own sons who had done them so much honor by his public service. And, as it has been my peculiar happiness to know, perhaps more than any of [the trustees], your usefulness in an important public station, on that and some other accounts, there was none to whom it gave greater satisfaction." Madison biographer Ralph Ketcham notes that Witherspoon influenced Madison's personal style of communication as well as its substance when the teacher advised his students to be modest and unassuming, as "nothing more certainly makes a man ridiculous than an over-forwardness to display his excellencies."[40] Madison's famous brevity of speech and conciseness of exposition may have come from Witherspoon's dictum: "Ne'er do ye speak unless ye ha' something to say, and when ye are done, be sure and leave off."[41]

Explicit historical evidence of theoretical influence is rare however; a political thinker or student seldom acknowledges direct ideological mentorship (Jefferson even *denied* the inspiration of Locke on his Declaration of Independence—in which it was most obvious). This is further complicated by the loss of Witherspoon's library and correspondence due to a fire. In Madison's time it was considered presumptuous or inappropriate to admit the influence of another, even a beloved teacher. But the conceptual similarities between Madison's political thought and that of his Princeton tutor are compelling.[42] To briefly summarize that philosophical affinity before examining it in depth, Witherspoon's conception of human nature as fallen and redeemed, as well as the necessity of a political structure of divided and balanced power, as a consequence of that nature, flow directly into Madison's political theory.

From Scripture and historical experience, Dr. Witherspoon concluded that human beings are sinful and depraved but capable, through the Spirit of Christ, of good actions. He finds in the Bible a "clear and consistent account of human depravity" in "opposition to the nature, and a transgression of the law of God."[43] This human depravity is passed on from Adam's disobedience to God, as the first man is the "federal" head of mankind. This means all humans are morally corrupt and are called to repentence and forgiveness through Christ. "Collateral" proof of this Augustinian view of humanity is the history of human war, selfishness, and cruelty.[44] Witherspoon insists, however, that the redemption of Christ and indwelling of God's Spirit in believers can ameliorate human evil, if not totally eliminate it. "I am none of those" Witherspoon wrote, "who either deny or conceal the depravity of human nature til it is purified by the light of truth, and renewed by the Spirit of the living God."[45] This view of a sinful human nature potentially redeemed through the saving grace of God is revealed in Madison's famous assessment of human nature in *Federalist* #51: "As there is a degree of depravity in mankind which requires a certain degree of circumspection and distrust; so there are other qualities in human nature, which justify a certain portion of esteem and confidence."[46]

This positive potential of humanity makes a republican form of government—self government—possible; but the lingering selfishness and evil in human beings commends a governmental structure that divides power, pitting interest against interest, "ambition against ambition."[47] Witherspoon urges that a republic "must be complex, so that one principle may check the other. . . . They must be so balanced, that when everyone draws to his own interest or inclination there must be an even poise upon the whole." He recommends an "enlarged system" that would provide such a "balance of power" in society and government identical to that found in Madison's most famous *Federalist* #10.[48]

Madison's insistence in *Federalist* #10 that "the latent causes of faction are thus sown in the nature of man . . . self-love . . . different leaders ambitiously contending for pre-eminence and power . . . more disposed to vex and oppress each other than to co-operate for their common good" and that the remedy is to "extend the sphere and . . . take in a greater variety of parties and interests [making] it less probable that a majority of the whole will have a common motive to invade the rights of other citizens"[49] echoes Witherspoon's essential political thought. As Professor Smylie put it, Madison translated his teacher's philosophy "into a responsible political structure" that recognized man's wicked tendencies without absolving him of his responsibilities.[50] Human evil may persist, but that neither excuses the individual from moral responsibility nor completely disqualifies him from goodness, as the Spirit of Christ is able to perform virtue through him.

Witherspoon apparently approved of Madison's adaptation of his ideas into the new constitution. A young faculty member at Princeton named Ashbel Green wrote that Witherspoon regarded the U.S. Constitution "as embracing principles and carrying into effect measures, which he had long advocated, as essential to the preservation of the liberties, and the promotion of the peace and prosperity of the country."[51] The political theory that Madison received from his master and mentor, as shown in Witherspoon's *Lectures on Moral Philosophy*, blended the three dominant ideologies of Revolutionary America: Calvinist Christianity, classical republicanism, and Lockean liberalism.

LOCKEAN LIBERALISM

Dr. Witherspoon displays a Lockean conception of politics as derived from a "social contract" formed by free individuals possessing natural rights to life, liberty, and property. In lecture 11, "Of Civil Society," Witherspoon says that "Civil Society . . . is the union of a number of families in one state, for their mutual benefit," and it implies "the consent of every individual" to the plan of government and the purpose of government: protection of private rights.[52] "The rights of subjects in a social state . . . may be summed up in *protection* . . . those who have surrendered part of their natural rights expect the strength of the public arm to defend and improve what remains."[53] In lecture 10, "Of Politics," Witherspoon summarizes his Lockean perspective of a limited, contractual government in this way: "Society I would define to be an association or compact of any number of persons, to deliver up or abridge some part of their natural rights, in order to have the strength of the united body, to protect the remaining, and to bestow others."[54]

To Witherspoon, the protection of liberty by the social contract promotes many useful human activities, conducted in a constructive and orderly way. "What then is the advantage of civil liberty? I suppose it chiefly consists in its tendency to put in motion all the human powers . . . it promotes industry, and in this respect happiness —produces every latent quality, and improves the human mind, —Liberty is the nurse of riches, literature and heroism" (147).

Yet even in his discussion of individual natural rights, Witherspoon's Christianity appears, as he insists that social relations are subordinate to one's relation to God: "The natural states may be enunciated thus: (1.) His state with regard to God . . . (2.) To his fellow creatures. (3.) Solitude or society. (4.) Peace or war . . . (5.) His outward provision, plenty or want. . . . All men, and at all times, are related to God. They were made by him, and live by his providence" (95). In typical Puritan fashion, for Witherspoon social contracts exist within God's Covenant.

CLASSICAL REPUBLICANISM

Dr. Witherspoon displays an acquaintance with classical republicanism, especially that of Aristotle, in his understanding of the different forms of government, their respective virtues, and the advantages of mixed regimes. In Lecture 12, "Of Civil Society," Witherspoon explains that "the ancients generally divided the forms of government" into "(1.) monarchy, (2.) aristocracy, (3.) democracy" (142).[55] Each regime, whether the rule of one, the few, or the many, Witherspoon notes, after Aristotle, has a specific strength or virtue, and each governmental form has a weakness or vice. Kingship has the advantage of unity and secrecy, but it is always potentially tyrannical and, if hereditary, provides "no security at all for either wisdom or goodness" (143).[56] Aristocracy, because of its small numbers and noble quality, "has the advantage of all the others for *wisdom* in deliberations . . . a number of persons of the first rank must be supposed by their consultations to be able to discover the public interest" (143). The peril of aristocratic governments is that they make "vassals of the inferior ranks, who have no hand in government" and "rule with greater severity than absolute monarchs" (144). Democracies allow the greatest number of citizens in ruling, Witherspoon notes, but often, as he learned from Aristotle, they degenerate into mob rule, "deceived by demagogues" and "subject to caprice and the madness of popular rage" (143–44).

The Aristotelian solution, of course, is the mixed regime, with elements of monarchy, aristocracy, and polity balancing one another for the most stable, just regime. "Hence," Witherspoon says, "it appears that every good form of government must be complex . . . must be so balanced, that when every one draws to his own interest or inclination, there may be an over poise upon the whole" (144). In other words, checks and balances. "A virtuous mind and virtuous conduct is possible" Witherspoon believes, "in every form of government" (147),[57] but the safest regime partakes of the advantages of each and counterbalances them. "Where there is a balance of different bodies, as in all mixed forms, there must be always some *nexus imperii*, something to make one of them necessary to the other. . . . In order to produce this *nexus*, some of the essential rights of rulers must be divided and distributed among the different branches" (144).

Yet, again, Witherspoon's classical republicanism is subordinated to his Christianity; the foundations of ancient political virtue are, for him, grounded in "(1.) The will of God. (2.) The reason and nature of things. (3.) The public interest. (4.) Private interest" (85). In summing up the relation of classical political wisdom to Christian truth, Witherspoon said in lecture 4: "The result of the whole is, that we ought to take the rule of duty from conscience enlightened by reason, experience, and every way by which we can be supposed to learn the will of our Maker, and his intention. . . . And we ought to believe that it is as deeply founded as the nature of God himself, being a transcript of his moral excellence, and that it is productive of the greatest good" (87). So, while Witherspoon draws upon both the British liberalism of Locke and the classical republicanism of Aristotle, both are subsumed within his Christianity, with its concern for discerning the will of God in earthly affairs and performing with humility all human goodness for the glory of God.

Dr. Witherspoon's *Lectures on Moral Philosophy*, as much as his explicitly theological writings and sermons, evince the underlying Christian perspective on ethics, politics, law (jurisprudence), and psychology as taught at eighteenth-century Princeton. He defines moral philosophy as "that branch of Science which treats of the principles and laws of Duty or Morals." Though he calls it "philosophy" because it relies more on "reason" (intellect) than "revelation" (Scripture), Witherspoon insists that this doesn't make the subject less religious; it is not, as New England Puritan Cotton Mather claimed, "reducing infidelity to a system." Rather, he finds that true reasoning and complete knowledge will never ultimately contradict Scripture. Indeed, they will confirm the truth of Christian revelation. "There is nothing certain or valuable in moral philosophy, but what is perfectly coincident with the Scripture, where the glory of God is the first principle of action" (64).

This Christian view and its implications for society, politics, and ethics remains the foundation of Witherspoon's teachings. How man's Maker created him (in God's image); how man's "depravity and corruption" led him to rebel against God and thereby separate himself from his creator; and how a loving Lord restored communion with His creation through the sacrifice of Jesus Christ and the gift of the Holy Spirit forms Witherspoon's conception of "the nature of man" and "the precise distinction between man and other animals" (187). From this Biblical perspective, human nature is shown to be a compound of "body and spirit," whose reciprocal influences reveal, for Witherspoon, the "infinite wisdom of the Creator" (66). From mankind's original disobedience to God's will come other "evil passions": sins of "ambition, envy, covetousness," which inflame hatred and destroy human relationships (70). At its worst, this sinful human nature leads to what he calls the "occult crimes" of murder, adultery, and forgery (71). In its milder expression, this human evil shows up in "profanity, impurity, violence and slander," but "in all polished nations" according to Witherspoon, "there are punishments annexed to the transgression of the moral laws, whether against God, our neighbor, or ourselves" (163).

The Bible says that even unredeemed man has been given a "conscience" by God wherewith to know the good, "the law which our Maker has written upon our hearts," which, Witherspoon notes, "intimates and enforces duty" (163). As St. Paul wrote in Romans 2:14–15 about this divinely ordained conscience: "For when the Gentiles, which have not the law, do by nature the things contained in the law, these having not the law, are a law unto themselves, which shew the work of the law written in their hearts, their consciences also bearing witness, and their thoughts the meanwhile accusing or else excusing one another." Witherspoon ascribes Frances Hutcheson's Scottish Enlightenment term *moral sense* to this Christian notion of "conscience," which allows even pagans to know right and wrong and achieve a certain social order and goodness based on family affection, friendship, and patriotism (78). This natural conscience cannot develop into perfection without the saving grace of God through accepting Christ and following His example; but it can contribute to a certain sense of order, decency, and proportion (71, 77–78). And, likewise, even those saved will be haunted by their "old nature" from time to time—tempted by sin and potentially displaying selfish passions: love of fame and the lust for power, property, and pleasure (73).[58] Hence, for Christians of Witherspoon's ilk, it is clear that society can never rely totally on any man, for they know, as Jesus did, "what is in man"—a continuing sinful selfishness and ambition, our righteousness being only in Christ (John 2:25). This has direct implications for Witherspoon's and Madison's political theory.

Even with Witherspoon's Calvinist Augustinian emphasis on human sin, he notes that the conscience gives all humans a knowledge of honor and shame, of ridicule and "inward remorse" (81) when one does evil (and to the Christian, it gives a heightened appreciation of God's grace and forgiveness). The fullest virtue and most consistent conscience is that which voluntarily seeks to know and follow God's will as revealed in scripture. "The divine will is so perfect and excellent, that all virtue is reduced to conformity to it—and that we ought not to judge of good and evil by any other rule."

Witherspoon also adds that "the divine conduct is the standard of wisdom" (85). The Christian believes that following divine example, by the power of the Holy Spirit, is the highest standard of human conduct. For Witherspoon, "the moral perfections of good are holiness, justice, truth, goodness and mercy" (102), and so our duty is "to obey him and submit to him in all things . . . considering every good action as an act of obedience to God." The "foundation of virtue," then, is "a sense of dependence and subjection to God" (103). We should love, fear, trust, worship, and praise. The duty of prayer (which for Witherspoon "has a real efficacy" [107]) should not be neglected. Hutcheson's Moral Sense School emphasized human benevolence, but Witherspoon argued that Jesus' Sermon on the Mount "carried benevolence to its greatest perfection" (109; Matt. 5:7, Luke 6:17). Love to others "is the sum of our duty" (109; Matt. 22:39). To Witherspoon, Jesus' parable of the Good Samaritan remained the best example of Godly conduct. Quoting Christ, love to God and love to man is the substance of religion; "where these prevail, civil laws will have little to do" according to Witherspoon (159). A magistrate ought to therefore "encourage piety by his own example" and "defend the rights of conscience . . . [as well as] tolerate all . . . religious sentiments that are not injurious to their neighbors" (160)[59] Madison's embracing of religious liberty (see chap. 2) reflects this concern for its efficacy in social order.

SIN AND POLITICS

The Calvinist theology that Dr. Witherspoon taught James Madison (coming after that of Madison's two Scottish tutors) was known for its emphasis on sin. Following the earlier Augustinian Christianity, this Protestant theology revived a concentration on man's fallen and sinful conditions, a reality that persisted throughout human history. It countered the more optimistic rationalism of St. Thomas Aquinas, who, like other late-Enlightenment thinkers, viewed reason as capable of overcoming evil. The reformed Christian emphasis on the persistence of sin directly influences the reformed Christian conception of politics. Man's pride, arrogance, and selfishness would always find expression in the power of the state, making most of political history a saga of violence, domination, and oppression. Even a Christian continues to "will that which is evil" by "reason of his remaining corruption," as the *Westminster Confession* (9:iv) insists.[60]

This Calvinist perspective on human evil draws from the Biblical portrayal of man's original sin. The fall of man described in the Book of Genesis relates Adam's sin as flowing from a God-given free will perverted by man's pride and arrogance. Disobedience to God's will (disobeying the command to not eat of the fruit of the tree "of the knowledge of good and evil") occasions the first, original sin, from which all other sins and crimes follow. Eve, with ample assistance from the serpent, or Satan, succumbs to an all-too-human pride to become more than she is intended to be, to be "like God," causing an expulsion from paradise and separation from God. From this act, the seed of humanity is cursed with death, pain, and evil.[61]

So, from this Biblical view, all human sins grow from this first original sin of disobedience to God and His will. The prophet Jeremiah wrote that "The heart is deceitful above all things and desperately wicked" (Jer. 17:9); and even Jesus said that "out of the heart proceed evil thoughts, murders, adulteries, fornications, thefts, false witness, blasphemies" (Matt. 15:19). Envy, greed, murder, lust, hatred, oppression of others, all follow from each person wanting to be God, expecting others to acknowledge that fact and denying the true Creator. The Bible recounts this in profusion: Cain killing Abel out of envy; King David having Uriah killed after committing adultery with his wife Bathsheba (and then crying "my sin is always before me" in Psalm 51 when the prophet Nathan confronts him with his deed); the prophet Isaiah preaching to Israel that "your iniquities have separated you from your God; your sins have hidden his face from you" (Isa. 59:2). For Christians like Witherspoon, it appears the Lord gives the Ten Commandments to His people through Moses, showing them Godly standards of life, and then watches them break one after another, making them deserving of God's wrath. St. Paul proclaims "there is no one righteous, not even one" (Rom. 3:10).

The appropriate punishment for this evil is death, a separation from the holy God who gives life and eternal condemnation to the hell which humans themselves have created. A holy God cannot commune with a proud, rebellious humanity. Christian doctrine proclaims that Jesus took the punishment for this sin upon Himself, on the cross, restoring humanity to God through faith in His act, God overcoming justice with mercy or "grace." "For God so loved the world that he gave his one and only Son, that whoever believes in him shall not perish but have eternal life" (John 3:16). It only remains for individual humans to acknowledge their sinful natures and repent, humbly accepting God's forgiveness through Christ. "If we claim to be without sin, we deceive ourselves and the truth is not in us. If we confess our sins, he is faithful and just to forgive us our sins and purify us from all unrighteousness" (1 John 1:8–9). But even Christians (at least in the Augustinian tradition) continue to sin in this life, requiring continual confession and repentance. Sinful humans resent this description of their condition; in their pride they think they are good. St. Augustine, to whom Witherspoon's Calvinism is so indebted, wrote:

> That the whole human race has been condemned in its first origin . . . bears witness by the host of cruel ills with which it is filled. Is not this proved by the profound and dreadful ignorance which produces all the errors that enfold the children of Adam, and from which no man can be delivered without toil, pain and fear? Is it not proved by his love of so many vain and hurtful things, which produces gnawing cares, disquiet, griefs, fears, wild joys, quarrels, law-suits, wars, treasons, angers, hatreds, deceit, flattery, fraud, theft, robbery, perfidy, pride, ambition, envy, murders . . . adulteries . . . sacrileges . . . oppression of the innocent . . . plots . . . violent deeds . . . and innumerable other crimes that . . . never absent themselves from the actuality of human existence? These are indeed the crimes of wicked men, yet they spring from that root of error and misplaced love which is born with every son of Adam.[62]

Such sin, for Augustine, may be for "every son of Adam," but the temptation to them is greater in the rich and powerful, the "worldly," arrogant human beings, who are made more confident in their own virtue and, therefore, more prone to the political manifestations of sin—the will to power, factional conflict, domination, and oppression. Hence Madison's concern with factions, political oppression, and injustice, and his remedy in American pluralism.

His political theory cannot be understood apart from this theology. Madison's familiarity with this Augustinian and reformed theology is evident in his choice of books for the religion section of the new University of Virginia's library, a list of which Thomas Jefferson asked him to provide. In Madison's catalog the Augustinian and Protestant writers predominate: early church fathers, St. Clement, Athenagoras, Tertullian, Irenaeus, St. Augustine, Martin Luther, John Calvin, Erasmus, Bellarmino and Chillingworth, John Wesley, Jonathan Edwards, William Penn, and Cotton Mather.[63]

John Calvin echoed the Augustinian emphasis on that persistent nature of human sin. In his *Institutes of the Christian Religion,* which served as a handbook for Puritan and Scottish Presbyterian churches, Calvin described the curse of sin in this way:

> Since blind self-love is innate in all mortals, they are most freely persuaded that nothing inheres in themselves that deserves to be considered hateful . . . the utterly vain opinion generally obtains credence that man is abundantly sufficient of himself to lead a good and blessed life. . . . Nothing pleases man more than the sort of alluring talk that tickles the pride that itches in his very marrow.[64]

The Bible presents, for Calvin, "a picture of human nature that showed us corrupt and perverted in every part." The prophet Jeremiah describes the human heart as "deceitful and corrupt above all else."[65] Calvin finds that "The venom of asps is under their lips [Ps. 140:3]; Their mouth is full of cursing and bitterness [Ps. 10:7]; Their feet are swift to shed blood; in their paths are ruin and misery [Isa. 59:7]; There is no fear of God before their eyes [Rom. 3:10–16]." Therefore, he writes, "good men (and Augustine above the rest) labored to show us that we are corrupted not by derived wickedness, but that we bear inborn defect from our mother's womb. To deny this was the height of shamefulness." And many people, "after they have become hardened in insolent and habitual sinning, furiously repel all remembrance of God."[66]

Witherspoon adopted this Calvinist view of human evil and depravity, and it informed his political theory. In his *Lectures on Moral Philosophy*, he maintains that this sinful nature and the pride it implies (sinful man resenting the acknowledgment of his own evil nature and need of a Savior and forgiveness) makes the philosophical discovery of human nature difficult. "Perhaps this circumstance itself," Witherspoon writes, "is a strong presumption of the truth of the Scripture doctrine of the depravity and corruption of our nature."[67] Witherspoon's sermon topics, such as "All Mankind by Nature under Sin" and "Christ's Death a Proper Atonement for Sin," confirm his Calvinist orthodoxy.[68]

James Madison, Witherspoon's most famous student at Princeton, adopted this Calvinist view of human nature: the predominance of sin, selfishness, and rebellion against God leading to man's domination of others, as well as the political implications of that nature. In the Episcopal church Madison attended every Sunday as he grew up in Virginia, the prayers and "confession of sin" are recited: "the Scripture moveth us . . . to acknowledge and confess our manifold sins and wickedness . . . confess them with an humble lowly, penitent, and obedient heart . . . Almighty and most merciful Father; We have erred, and strayed from thy ways like lost sheep . . . we have offended against thy holy laws . . . and there is no health in us."

Madison expresses this Christian concern over the sinful nature of mankind when, in *Federalist* #55 he writes that the "depravity in mankind" requires a "distrust" of everything he does, especially in politics. To his Princeton classmate William Bradford, Madison wrote of the "emptiness of Earthly Happiness"; its "allurements and vanities" requiring Christians to acknowledge the "follies of mankind" and frame their lives according to "the precepts of Wisdom and Religion."[69] In deciding on a career he notes, "a watchful eye must be kept on ourselves lest while we are building ideal monuments of Renown and bliss here we neglect to have our names enrolled in the Annals of Heaven." Showing his preference for simple, virtuous rural life, Madison asserts that cities especially abound in "food enough for [man's] Vanity and impertinence."[70] And political power affords the greatest temptations for human weakness, which requires a system of government that pits "ambition against ambition" (that is, checks and balances) and will acknowledge man's "imperfections and weaknesses," which historically have caused "quarrels, jealousies, and envy" prompted by humans' "love of pre-eminence" and "wounded pride," leading to political "vindictiveness." The seeds of political faction, for Madison, are "sown in the [sinful] nature of man."[71] Along with Alexander Hamilton, he commends the federalists' constitutional realism, which "never expects a perfect work from imperfect man." This "experience of the ages" made the founders realize that America is, like every other nation, "remote from the happy empire of perfect wisdom and perfect virtue."[72]

Elsewhere in his political writings, Madison again expresses this Christian suspicion of human nature and human motives. He refers to the "follies of mankind"; the "vanity and impertinence" of cities; and the "vices" of the Articles of Confederation. He characterizes the French ally Lafayette as motivated by "personal glory" and "vanity" and notes that his own reluctance to serve free liquor during an election campaign was attributed to "pride or parsimony."[73] The territorial conflicts among states Madison ascribes to "envy and jealousy"; hearing a rumor that Benjamin Franklin, just before the American Revolutionary War, had turned traitor, Madison wrote "little did I ever expect to hear that Jeremiah's Doctrine that 'the heart of man is deceitful above all things and desperately wicked'" would apply to the Philadelphian.[74] The reality of human pride and sin meant that "wherever there is an interest and power to do wrong, wrong will generally be done," and, sadly, "conscience . . . is known to be inadequate in individuals" to overcome it. Madison warned that even "religion itself may become a motive to persecution and oppression," as human sin and pride can find expression in doctrinal and spiritual forms.[75]

So, Madison's Calvinist convictions, with their emphasis on human sin and weakness, underlie his application of other political philosophies, notably Lockean liberalism and classical republicanism, to the American political reality.[76]

After Madison's graduate studies in theology and Hebrew with Dr. Witherspoon at Princeton, he returned to his family estate at Montpelier in 1772. For two years he pursued his "customary enjoyments Solitude and Contemplation."[77] Partly because of ill health, but also suiting his bookish nature, Madison spent the years just prior to the American Revolution in study. As political events in the colonies intensified, Madison resumed his investigations of government: historical regimes, ancient and modern; legal and political philosophy, and the relationship between religion and statecraft. He wrote to his Princeton classmate William Bradford that "the principles and Modes of Government are too important to be disregarded by an Inquisitive mind and I think are well worthy a critical examination by all students that have health and leisure."[78] He may not have had health, but he did have leisure. Yet even then, while studying the history and principles of government, Madison found himself being drawn into the real turmoil of Virginia politics, inflamed by the impending revolution. Still, Madison's response to emerging political issues and events were always viewed through his earlier intellectual experience.

CHAPTER TWO

POLITICS AND RELIGION

That diabolical Hell. . . of persecution.
—James Madison, 1773

IRONICALLY, THE FIRST public issue that Madison faced upon returning to Virginia from Princeton was the domination of religion by politics, specifically, the odd connection of religious faith to law that existed in colonial Virginia. As a royalist colony, the "Old Dominion," which remained loyal to King Charles I during the Puritan Revolution in England, maintained the established Anglican Church as the only legally valid Christian denomination. As in Britain, the Church of England in Virginia enjoyed exclusive status in the Commonwealth: it was funded by state taxes; it enforced church attendance by threat of imprisonment or fine; and it persecuted dissenting ministers and believers with jail sentences and public humiliation. The effect of this official, imperial church was literally, for Madison, the destruction of Christianity. The state religion encouraged the sins of pride and arrogance in its supporters and condoned the use of unchristian methods of conversion—threats and violence rather than prayer and persuasion.

It was said that Madison never forgot the sight of a Baptist minister in Culpeper, Virginia, preaching to a small group of his flock through the bars of his prison cell.[1] This conjured up for some a vision of early Christians dragged before Roman officials, ordered to make sacrifices to the state gods and then executed when they refused.[2] An oppressive established church actually persecuted Christians, in Madison's view. Having learned a Biblical faith and having witnessed a vital Christianity during revivals at Princeton, Madison thought the Anglican hierarchy in Virginia was as contrary to the true faith as those earlier Roman pagan practices. The clergy were lax and decadent, the seminary was corrupt and lifeless, the liturgy was proud and worldly, services were cold and lifeless, and the essential teachings of Christ were hidden behind a mountain of meaningless ritual and vague teaching. The Christian virtues of love, humility, and faith were belied by a proud, dignified, and immoral clergy, aligned with a dictatorial, imperial regime.

Like the official Medieval Catholic Church or, later, the Russian Orthodox Church, religious institutions that became part of the government soon became as arrogant and worldly as the state itself. Their values soon became those of the world: social power, riches, and prestige. No longer recognizable as the Church of Jesus Christ, instead Virginia's state religion had devolved into a dead, formal, officious, proud, and corrupt institution that excluded the purity of Christian love and faith. This was, for Madison, worse than the pagan authorities that had persecuted Christians because now this persecution was being done in the name of Christ; it was, as he saw it, a "diabolical Hell."

Only the elimination of the official state church and the reestablishment of freedom of religious conscience could restore Christianity to Virginia in its vital, life-changing form. The true Church of Jesus Christ would only flourish in a free environment, unfettered by legal restrictions. Madison's tutor at Princeton, John Witherspoon, had written that the "knowledge of God and his truths have from the beginning . . . been confined to those parts of the earth where some degree of liberty and political justice were to be seen. . . . knowledge of divine truth . . . has been spread by liberty."[3] Following St. Paul's dictum, Madison may have thought of the Virginians, "How then shall they call on him in whom they have not believed? And how shall they believe in him of whom they have not heard? and how shall they hear without a preacher?" (Rom. 10:14). If the indolent Episcopal ministers were not preaching Christ and were not giving an example of the humble, patient, loving Christian life, Virginians could only get it from the "dissenting" (Presbyterian, Baptist, Brethren) ministers; and for them to be heard would require freedom of religion. "Faith cometh by hearing, and hearing by the word of God" (Rom. 10:17) was the Virginia evangelical's favorite Bible verse regarding the church and the need for religious liberty. The faith and virtue of Virginians were weak because they had no church to preach the Word to them, owing to an established church which excluded those evangelical churches that faithfully taught Christ. Since the faith and virtue of the people would directly affect their social and political virtue, Madison saw religious freedom as essential to a virtuous American republic. The unshackling of religious truth therefore would be required for Republican virtue.

Madison revealed these sentiments in correspondence with classmate William Bradford soon after returning home from college. In 1773 he asked Bradford for documents on the government of his native Pennsylvania, especially those relating to "religious Toleration."[4] Later, he praised the "free Air" of religious liberty in the Mid-Atlantic region and declared that if all the American colonies had the established Anglican Church of Virginia, the whole continent would be in moral and religious slavery. "If the Church of England had been established and general Religion in all the Northern Colonies as it has been among us here and uninterrupted tranquility had prevailed throughout the Continent, it is clear to me that slavery and subjection might and would have been gradually insinuated among us" (28). The Puritan churches of New England and the diverse, if predominantly Calvinist, churches of the Mid-Atlantic region fomented the revolutionary cause in America.

By contrast, Madison insisted, "Ecclesiastical Establishments tend to great ignorance [of Christianity] and Corruption [of faith]" and "facilitate the Execution of mischievous Projects [in] politics" (28). Christianity in Virginia, Madison lamented, was characterized by "Pride, ignorance and Knavery among the Priesthood and Vice and Wickedness among the Laity." The official state church actually persecuted Christians—suppressing vital, faithful churches which strive to carry on the work of the gospel and evangelists. "That diabolical Hell conceived principle of persecution rages" in Madison's Virginia of 1774, and "to their eternal Infamy the [established] Clergy can furnish their Quote of Imps for such business," Madison complained (29). He wrote that the most horrifying aspect of this was the presence of five or six ministers of the Gospel in jail "for publishing their religious Sentiments which in the main are very ortho-dox" (i.e., Baptists). He ended this letter to Bradford by asking him to "pray for Liberty of Conscience" so the truth of Christianity can be preached freely in Virginia (29).

Four months later, Madison told his old Princeton friend that petitions to the Virginia legislature were expected from the perse-cuted Christians; but he was doubtful there would be any loosening of the state laws. The established Anglican clergy influencing the legislature had told such "incredible and extravagant stories" of the "enthusiasm" of evangelical revival services (reporting wild shout-ing, dancing, weeping, and falling down during revivalist preach-ing) that they had convinced the majority to continue the official state church, with its order and decorum. And, Madison wrote, "the Clergy are a numerous and powerful body" who had "connec-tion with and dependence on the Bishops and Crown," so they "naturally employ all their art and interest to depress their rising Adversaries," the dissenting Baptist and Presbyterian ministers who "endanger their livings and security" (30).

This seemed a clear case of human sin hiding behind clerical gowns, a corrupt church serving Mammon rather than God. Such "Religious bondage," Madison complained, "shackles and debili-tates the mind and unfits it for every noble enterprize." He con-trasted this with the regions of America where freedom of religion promoted a lively, honest Christian faith and practice, where the "public has long felt the good effects of their religious as well as Civil Liberty." In such areas where true Christianity has flourished, "Industry and Virtue have been promoted by mutual emulation and mutual inspection" of the different Christian denominations, and "Commerce and the Arts have flourished," unlike in the dead and decadent culture of Anglican Virginia. "That liberal catholic and equitable way of thinking as to the rights of Conscience . . . is but little known among the zealous adherents to our Hierarchy," Madison lamented (30).

Madison got his first chance to end the persecution of Christians in Virginia when he was elected to the new state legislature in 1776. He was appointed to a committee to prepare a Declaration of Rights and a new constitution for the Commonwealth of Virginia. The committee, under the leadership of George Mason, approached ending the domination of the Anglican establishment by adopting a draft resolution that "all men should enjoy the fullest toleration in the exercise of Religion."[5] This implied that the official religion would continue, as in England, but dissenting churches (like Baptists and Presbyterians) would be "tolerated," that is, no longer prosecuted under the law. Madison proposed an alternative clause, replacing the word *toleration* (and the state religion it implied) with the wording: "all men are equally entitled to the full and free exercise of [religion] according to the dictates of conscience" (72). This threatened the Anglican establishment enough to cause the resolution's defeat in the Virginia legislature. Madison then proposed a more general amendment, which, while not directly attacking the establishment, endorsed liberty of conscience and Christian forbearance: "That religion, or the duty which we owe our Creator, and the manner of discharging it, can be directed only by reason and conviction, not by force or violence; and therefore, all men are equally entitled to the free exercise of religion, according to the dictates of conscience; and that the mutual duty of all to practice Christian forbearance, love, and charity towards each other" (73). This resolution expressed the spirit of religious liberty that the evangelical Christians needed, even if it didn't change the letter of the law that continued an official state religion.

At the following session of the Virginia legislature, Madison was placed on the Committee on Religion, better allowing him to continue his efforts on behalf of persecuted Christians. The Committee immediately began receiving petitions from Presbyterians in Virginia calling for the end of the established Anglican Church and their "long night of Ecclesiastical bondage." They beseeched the legislature that "without delay, all Church establishments . . . be pulled down, and every tax upon conscience and private judgement be abolished" so that Virginia could enjoy "the virtuous of every denomination" (75). The Virginia Presbyterians had been at the forefront of the lively Great Awakening revivals, and they especially suffered from the dead, formal Anglican liturgical style and resented the dismal prospect of paying taxes to support such a moribund church. The Committee on Religion reported out principles abolishing the old British statutes of religious bigotry, eliminating dissenters' requirement to pay taxes supporting the state church, and arguing against state payment of Anglican clergy salaries—effectively disestablishing the Episcopal Church. The legislature nevertheless allowed the Anglican establishment to retain its vast land and property holdings and suspended tax-supported salaries for only one year; but the public funding of Episcopal clergy salaries was never reinstated, so this session did in effect bring down the state church in Virginia. In the new, independent Commonwealth of Virginia, state persecution of Christians ended and the evangelical churches were able to flourish.

Another attempt to reinstate political domination of religion occurred in the 1780s, when Madison was again in legislature; but after his 1776 term he was defeated as delegate for reelection from his County of Orange. In a later autobiographical account, Madison attributed this defeat to his refusal to abide by the normal custom of providing free liquor at campaign rallies. Regarding this practice (which apparently predated Jefferson's Democratic Party) as "inconsistent with the purity of moral and republican principles," Madison found his moral stance "being represented as the effect of pride or parsimony" by the local constituents (77). This "sobering reality" of a "licentious people" (153, 154) may have confirmed his Calvinist view of human nature and increased his desire for the free spread of Christianity in Virginia, especially the Baptist variety, which preached against the evils of liquor and urged the repentance of drunkards. It didn't help that his victorious opponent was Charles Porter, a local tavern keeper.

Despite his electoral defeat, the Virginia General Assembly obviously still valued Madison's public contributions, since it immediately elected him to the Governor's Council of State, a powerful executive body on which he served with seven other prominent leaders from 1777 to 1779 (78). Oddly enough, he probably had more influence and prestige on the Governor's Council than he had enjoyed as a delegate from Orange County.

Madison's efforts at freeing Christianity from state restrictions were continued in Virginia when he returned to the legislature in 1784. That year, the idea of an official state-supported religion resurfaced with Patrick Henry's proposal for a general tax or "assessment" to support "teachers of the Christian religion"—all clergy whom the government determined were ministers of the Christian church, broadly defined. The proposal was supported by many prominent leaders, including George Washington, Edmund Pendleton, Richard Henry Lee, John Marshall, and Benjamin Harrison, under the principle that religion was essential to the well-being of society and necessary to cure the "moral decay" experienced in the Commonwealth during the Revolutionary War. Madison, on the other hand, found this proposal "obnoxious on account of its dishonorable principle and dangerous tendency" (162–63). While he agreed that a Christian culture in Virginia would promote public virtue and private morality, he predicted that giving the state jurisdiction over determining which ministers were "Christian" and thereby eligible for governmental support would again, like the Episcopal establishment, corrupt the church, damage the truth of Christian revelation, and therefore ultimately harm social ethics and individual morals. So, during the next break in the legislative session, he composed the "Memorial and Remonstrance against Religious Assessments," providing his classic argument for religious freedom and liberty of conscience.

The first argument in the famous "Memorial and Remonstrance" echoes the Virginia Declaration of Rights in asserting that "religion or the duty which we owe to our creator and the manner of discharging it, can be directed only by reason and conviction, not by force or violence . . . [it] must be left to the conscience of every man. . . . It is the duty of every man to render to the Creator such homage and such only as he believes to be acceptable to him."[6] Civil society, Madison adds, has no right to impose a certain religious belief on an individual citizen, even if the majority subscribe to it, because "religion is wholly exempt from its cognizance." The decadent and truncated religion of the Anglican establishment, which suppressed lively, vital Christianity, must have been in Madison's mind when he wrote that "the same authority which can establish Christianity in exclusion of all other religions, may establish with the same ease any particular sect of Christians, in exclusion of all other sects" (92). His dread of the return of those official Christian churches that oppressed the true faith made the religious assessment as disturbing to Madison as the old Church of England. With official sanction and support, the church would again become proud and worldly, dignified and arrogant, unworthy of the Christ who regarded the meek as blessed.

Madison believed that the individual, not governments, would have to answer to God for neglecting the true faith. "Whilst we assert for ourselves a freedom to embrace, to profess and to observe the Religion [Christianity] which we believe to be of divine origin, we cannot deny an equal freedom to those whose minds have not yet yielded to the evidence which has convinced us." In an atmosphere of religious freedom, the burden of searching for religious truth and God's will rests on the individual creature of God, where it belongs. "If this freedom be abused" by the individual who neglects the search for God or the duty to honor and revere Christ, "it is an offense against God, not against man: To God, therefore, not to man, must an account of it be rendered" (93). In this twist on Jesus' command to "render unto to Caesar that which is Caesar's, and unto God that which is God's" (Matt. 22:21), Madison shows that society is responsible to ensure that the true faith is available for all to see and freely accept or reject, a duty best accomplished in an environment of religious liberty.

The official churches, according to Madison, have always discredited Christ's teachings by employing "an unhallowed perversion of the means of salvation." State regulation of Christianity, he insisted, "is a contradiction to the Christian Religion itself, for every page of it [Christianity] disavows a dependence on the powers of this world." Historically, Madison asserted, the Christian faith has "both existed and flourished, not only without the support of human laws, but in spite of every opposition from them . . . not only during the period of miraculous aid [the early church], but long after it had been left to its own evidence and the ordinary care of Providence" (93). The spirit of God that flowed over the Mediterranean region, Asia Minor, and Europe, causing massive conversions to Christ in the first three centuries of the church, not only did not need the support of the Roman government, it succeeded in spite of fierce persecution by the government.

Once the state began supporting the Christian church, it assumed control and was able to use the church for its own worldly purposes, effectively corrupting the church. "Experience witnesseth that ecclesiastical establishments, instead of maintaining the purity and efficacy of religion, have had a contrary operation," Madison pointed out. As in the case of the Anglican establishment in Virginia, the "fruits" of all state churches have been "pride and indolence in the Clergy, ignorance and servility in the Laity . . . [and] superstition and bigotry." The light of Christ shone "in its greatest luster," Madison exclaimed, "prior to its incorporation with Civil policy," when ministers, with the help of God, depended on the voluntary support of their flocks (93). State churches have invariably erected a spiritual tyranny "upholding the thrones of political tyranny." The assessment bill, Madison concludes in the "Memorial and Remonstrance," differs from the Spanish Inquisition only in degree, and it stood as "a signal of persecution" of many Christians (94). It would create "a monster feeding and thriving on its own venom, gradually swell[ing] to a size and strength overwhelming all laws human and divine."[7]

Madison's arguments in the "Memorial and Remonstrance" rallied the antiestablishment forces in Virginia, who successfully defeated the religious assessment bill. This victory was capped with the passage of Jefferson's Bill for Establishing Religious Freedom, which guaranteed liberty of conscience and formed the basis for the religious freedom clause of the First Amendment of the U.S. Constitution.[8]

The effect of religious liberty in Virginia confirmed Madison's assertion that Christianity was most vibrant and healthy in a free environment. Forty years later he wrote: "there has been an increase of religious instruction since [then]. . . . Religious instruction is now diffused throughout the community by preachers of every sect with almost equal zeal . . . and at private houses and open stations . . . the zeal which actuates them, the purity of their lives and the attendance of the people on their instructions."[9] Almost sixty years later, at the age of eighty-three, Madison wrote to Jasper Adams in response to his sermon "The Relation of Christianity to Civil Government," saying that the only issue was whether "the best and Purest religion, the Christian religion itself," was better advanced by government support or by complete freedom, and he quickly concluded it was the latter.[10] As historian Gordon Wood recently showed, the effect of religious freedom in the early republic was not the decline of Christianity but the Second Great Awakening—a religious revival that spread across the frontier in the early nineteenth century and effectively "christened" the United States as the most Evangelical Christian nation in the modern world.[11]

The dire predictions of Madison's opponents that the end of state-controlled religion would doom the church proved wrong, while his prophecy that Christianity would flourish in liberty became reality. In his long public career, he never again encountered "the diabolical Hell" of religious persecution, but Madison soon ran up against other forms of human pride and weakness as he moved to national politics in the Continental Congress.

CHAPTER THREE

FEDERALIST NATIONALISM

*The practice of many states . . . is certainly adverse to the
spirit of the Union.*

—James Madison, 1787

DURING JAMES MADISON'S "Nationalist Decade" (1780–89) in
Congress, he experienced ample evidence of the human depravity of
which the Calvinist Christian philosophy at Princeton had warned
him. Many weak, narrow, and selfish individuals crossed Madison's
path both inside and outside of government: petty and suspicious
state government personnel, treacherous enemies and manipulative
allies, and a fickle fiancée. While all of these may have confirmed an
Augustinian suspicion of human nature as self-interested and envi-
ous, of people easily offended and untrustworthy, this worldview
instead manifested itself in Madison's political writings as Lockean
liberalism (with its concern for individual natural rights and opposition to community encroachment) and nationalist federalism (with
its opposition to the conflict and disunion of states' rights). For
Madison, the greatest evil, or manifestation of human weakness, at
this point in history was the parochial interests of local communities, which violated individual rights.

Madison joined the Continental Congress in Philadelphia in
1780, during the height of the American Revolutionary War. There
he experienced personally the enormous difficulties of coordinating
a war effort under the impotent central government of the Articles
of Confederation, which left all real sovereignty in the states and
gave Congress no means for supplying the army, negotiating treaties,

or raising revenues unless all thirteen colonies unanimously approved the new measure. Having the responsibility for managing the nation's war effort without the authority to practically carry it out was tremendously frustrating for Madison. Madison, who was the youngest Congressional representative at age twenty-nine (and looked even younger with his frail, thin appearance and short stature) felt keenly the pain of trying to serve the nation's interests without the practical, institutional, or financial means of doing so. He himself received his Congressional salary so infrequently that he was forced to borrow money regularly from a Philadelphia Jewish lender, Haym Saloman, in order to pay his own rent and board.[1] To Madison, this humiliation was minor, however, compared to the national humiliation of poorly paid soldiers, inadequate regulation of trade, inflationary currency, and interstate conflict and social disorder. As Madison wrote to Jefferson in March 1780, summarizing the situation:

> Our army threatened with an immediate alternative of disbanding or living on free quarter; the public treasury empty; public credit exhausted; . . . Congress complaining of the extortion of the people; the people of the improvidence of Congress, and the army of both; our affairs requiring the most mature systematic measures, and the urgency of occasions admitting only of temporizing expedients.[2]

The primary culprit in these difficulties lay in the recalcitrant and independent state governments, which refused to fund the national government adequately or delegate authority to Congress over national matters. "If the states do not vigorously proceed in collecting the old money and establishing funds for the credit of the new, . . . we are undone," Madison lamented. Ironically, given the circumstances, he unfavorably compared Congressional dependence on the states to the King of England's dependence on the British Parliament.[3] About the same time, General Washington made similar observations on the dilemma of a national campaign being funded by a disunified collection of disparate states: "I see one head gradually changing into thirteen . . . I see the powers of Congress declining too fast for the consideration and respect which is due to them as the grand representative body of America, and am fearful of the consequences."[4] Those consequences, Madison reported to Jefferson in May 1780, were becoming increasingly alarming:

> Our army has as yet been kept from starving, and public measures from total stagnation, by draughts on the states for the unpaid requisitions. . . . A punctual compliance on the part of the states with the specific supplies will indeed render much less money necessary than would otherwise be wanted, but experience by no means affords satisfactory encouragement that due and unanimous exertions will be made for that purpose . . . our distress is so pressing that it is uncertain whether any exertions of that kind can give relief in time.[5]

This "sin" of states not paying their financial obligations to the central government and Congress's lack of power to compel them could lead to disastrous consequences—the failure of the Revolution, enslavement to Britain, and greater political oppression than before the war. Penurious states could cause the loss of all political liberty. In October 1780, Madison wrote to Joseph Jones that "we continue to receive periodical alarms from the Commissary's and Quarter Master's departments . . . our army is living hand to mouth . . . unless the states unanimously make a vigorous and speedy effort to form magazines . . . unless the states take other methods to procure their specific supplies . . . their utmost efforts to comply with the requisitions of Congress can be only a temporary relief." The only long-term answer, Madison believed, was for the central government to obtain the power to independently tax the citizens of the states for the common interest of conducting the war effort and winning political independence. Even then, he wrote, "taxation alone is inadequate"; borrowing from domestic and foreign lenders would still be required, as would the national power to secure such loans.[6] Centralized political authority, he determined, was necessary for the nation's survival.

Adding to young Madison's appreciation of the absurdity of America's attempts to conduct national policy without a true national regime was his service on the Continental Congress's Board of Admiralty, which attempted to oversee the equipping of an almost nonexistent navy. The board wrote to an officer commanding four small vessels seeking to guard Charleston, South Carolina, from a massive British fleet; it wrangled endlessly with agents in Boston over disposition of prizes captured by privateers and continually faced insubordination from naval officers.[7] It appeared ridiculous to Madison to attempt a national effort with a multitude of petty, selfish states and individual social entities. Private enterprises and local communities treated the national government with contempt.

Even before independence was won, the states and various land agents were fighting over the spoils of war, quarreling about the Western land claims that would be deeded to America after separation from Great Britain. Greed and jealousy, human sins that Madison's Calvinism emphasized, marred the war effort from the start. Madison wrote in May 1782 that "the territorial claims, particularly those of Virginia, are opposed by Rhode Island, New Jersey, Pennsylvania, Delaware and Maryland . . . by the envy and jealousy naturally excited by superior resources and importance . . . [and] the intrigues of their citizens who are interested in the claims of land companies. . . . The claim of New York is very extensive, but its title very flimsy."[8] Dividing up bountiful spoils, even before they had been won, aggravated human greed and hatred. Again, Madison saw that only a strong national tribunal could adequately adjudicate these competing interests and successfully protect valid rights to land ownership in the West while preserving the national interests of justice and social harmony.

Closely related to the mediation of conflicting state claims was the overall strength of the economy and its medium of currency. The inflation that plagued wartime America reflected, for Madison, the states' shortsighted self-interest, exacerbated by parochial suspicions; it could be ameliorated only by a strong, stable national currency, worthy of public confidence and capable of dampening human fears over financial insecurity.

The value of money, Madison wrote, was not dependent on its quantity but on the public confidence in its redeemability—that is, the perceived security of the issuing authority or government. Lack of confidence in America's central government had caused the Congressional currency to be devalued until it was virtually worthless. This provided yet another example, for Madison, of humankind's greed and fear and reaffirmed his conviction that a strong, stable central government was the only solution for this evil. He proposed a financial system of foreign loans to America, increased domestic taxes, and rigorous public economy.[9] The stability of a sound currency could quiet the anxiety of a weak, selfish citizenry and reduce the panic of social insolvency.

Foreign loans and military support for American independence raised other problems for Madison, however: namely, the tendency of allies to blackmail the United States, giving assistance only under exorbitant conditions that rendered independence almost a fiction. The terms of Spain's involvement on America's side is a good example. After the French and Indian War, Britain maintained the eastern bank of the Mississippi River, holding full navigation rights; Spain controlled the west bank and the mouth to the sea, at New Orleans. After declaring independence, America assumed continued navigation rights on the Mississippi. Spanish allegiance with the United States in 1779 came with their expectation of increased control over the river all the way to Louisiana. France sided with Spain and tried to persuade the Continental Congress to relinquish American rights to this water trade route.[10] Meanwhile, the western land claims that various states and companies were already fighting over were greatly affected in value by the legal status of that river.

Madison argued strenuously for the complete American right of navigation on the Mississippi River, which bordered the new nation. He claimed that terms of the Treaty of Paris (1763), negotiated by George III, devolved to the sovereign North American government and that Rights of Nature confirmed this worldly agreement.[11] In a congressional report advising the American ambassador to Spain, John Jay, Madison wrote a carefully reasoned treatise on Natural Law in international relations. He noted several reasons the Mississippi River should remain under U.S. control: it was "a more natural . . . more precise boundary than any other that can be drawn eastwardly," and therefore would be an appropriate line between countries; American citizens were much closer to settling the area than Spaniards; several states already claimed territory adjoining the river, so Congress, under the Articles of Confederation, could not relinquish that land or its usefulness; allowing a foreign government's rights over American citizens in the region would violate "the common rights of mankind"; and, finally, resources in the Mississippi valley could be put to better use by Americans than by Spaniards. Therefore, he stated, Spain's regulation of river navigation via the mouth at New Orleans would "contravene the clear indications of nature and providence, and the general good of mankind." Benjamin Franklin compared Spanish restrictions on Mississippi trade to a neighbor asking him "to sell [his] street door."[12] Madison later observed that Spain, as the heart of European Catholicism, monarchy, and the Inquisition, was the most uncongenial neighbor to the United States, one "whose government, religion and manners unfit them, of all nations in Christendom for a coalition with this country."[13]

America's other ally, France, was causing other difficulties during negotiations with Great Britain, demonstrating to Madison once again the evil and duplicity of human nature, especially where financial bounty and personal prestige were involved. French intrigue and dishonesty (along with the nation's image of persistent immorality) fueled factional disputes within America, wasting valuable energy in the Continental Congress which could have been better reserved for fighting the British Empire. An American commissioner in Paris, Arthur Lee, accused fellow commissioner Silas Deane of collusion with several Frenchmen in defrauding the United States of payment for arms and supplies that had been intended as a free gift. Deane, supported by Franklin, insisted that although diplomacy with France was inevitably corrupt and scandalously profitable, in the long run it was useful to America and the best arrangement possible.[14]

Lee then attacked Franklin for neglecting his public duty in France, profiteering through his nephew and a French banker, tolerating British Tories and spies, and living such a decadent and immoral lifestyle in Paris that it was "more devoted to pleasure than would become even a young man in his station."[15] Franklin's affinity for French brothels and courtier life led more restrained American diplomats to question his honesty, probity, and patriotism. John Adams joined this chorus against Franklin's methods, triggering the formation of an anti-French faction in America that lasted well into the early nineteenth century. Madison's realism (when in France, do as the French do) led him to support Franklin's exertions, while he also tried to placate Franklin's opponents in order to prevent a factious breech in Congress and the American war effort. He wrote

Edmund Pendleton, saying "Doctor Lee [and his colleagues] . . . have been here some time, and I believe are not very reserved in their reflections on the Venerable Philosopher [Franklin] at the Court of Versailles . . . I have had great anxiety lest the flame of faction . . . be kindled." Adams's critical letters from Paris especially disturbed Madison, who told Jefferson that they were "not remarkable for anything unless it be a display of [his] vanity, his prejudice against the French Court, and his venom against Doctor Franklin." Jefferson replied sympathetically, saying of Adams: "He hates Franklin, he hates Jay, he hates the French, he hates the English. . . . His dislike of all parties, and all men, by balancing his prejudices, may give the same fair play to his reason as would a general benevolence of temper. At any rate honesty may be extracted even from poisonous weeds."[16] Jefferson's prescience of "balancing" Adams's various negative attitudes into something equivalent to general benevolence may have contributed to Madison's later federalist argument for the benefits of many countervailing factions in ensuring social good.

If difficult relations with allies were not enough to confirm Madison's opinions of man's wicked tendencies, the conduct of the enemy provided numerous instances of human frailty and evil. The "barbarism" of the British troops during the American Revolution truly shocked Madison. In July of 1781 he wrote in a report to Philip Mazzei that "no description can give you an adequate idea of the barbarity with which the enemy have conducted the war in the Southern states. Every outrage which humanity could suffer has been committed by them. Desolation rather than conquest seems to be their object. . . . Rapes, murders and the whole catalogue of individual cruelties, not protection and the distribution of justice are the acts which characterize the sphere of their usurped jurisdiction." British savagery later gave way to British duplicity in the final peace treaty proposal, in which His Majesty's government included a secret article on the Florida boundary in an attempt to lure the United States into betraying its French and Spanish allies.[17] Madison observed that the American peace negotiators had been "ensnared by the dexterity of the British Ministries . . . writing sentiments unfriendly to our Ally" and serving "the insidious policy of the Enemy . . . as a means of disuniting the United States and France."[18] Only Britain's treacherous conduct exceeded the corrupt, manipulative behavior of America's friends and allies, indicating, for Madison, that betrayal and deceit abounded.

Madison's political realism not only permitted him to overlook Franklin's personal immorality and financial improprieties in France for the higher object of winning the Revolutionary War, it also allowed him to accept the monetary machinations of Robert Morris. Though he was certainly corrupt and self-serving, Morris's extensive and interrelated business dealings in land speculation, armaments, credit, and trade made it possible for him, as American Finance Director, to provide the only financial solvency possible in order to support the war effort to any successful degree amid such a weak central government. Madison thought Morris operated within acceptable limits, given the evil of human nature and the extremities of the time. "I own I cannot invent an excuse for the prepense malice [of purists] with which the character and services of this man are murdered. I am persuaded that he accepted his office from motives which were honorable and patriotic. I have seen no proof of malfeasance. . . . Every member in Congress must be sensible of the benefit which has accrued to the public from his administration."[19] Madison's appreciation of the reality of human frailty allowed him to hate the mixed moral motives of a Franklin or Morris less than he hated those of his "pure," self-righteous republican brethren, Lee and Adams.

Morris's services, and whatever corruption came with them, were rendered obligatory because the central government was unable to manage its financial affairs effectively. Therefore Madison continually strove to increase the authority of the national government, hoping to bring it to the level requisite to the contingencies of a war effort, international negotiations, and a national economy. After a mere twelve days of government under the Articles of Confederation, Madison proposed an amendment to strengthen the national government so it could manage the exigencies of the war. He urged "a general and implied power vested in the United States in Congress assembled to enforce and carry into effect all the Articles of the said Confederation against any of the states which Shall refuse or neglect to abide by such their determinations." Madison justified this compulsion of states' obedience to the wartime needs of the Union in a letter to Jefferson in April 1781:

The necessity of arming Congress with coercive powers arises from the shameful deficiency of some of the states which are most capable of yielding their appointed supplies, and the military exactions to which others already exhausted by the enemy and our own troops are in consequence exposed. Without such powers too in the general government, the whole confederacy may be insulted and the most salutary measures frustrated by the most inconsiderable state in the Union [i.e., Rhode Island]."[20]

For Madison, the chief problem at this time was the petty resistance of state government to support national control over foreign affairs, or America's external relations in the international arena— policy that had to be unified to be viable. Witnessing the defeat of nationalist amendments to the Articles of Confederation, he became more shrewd in expanding congressional authority, achieving the "minor" adjustments of giving Congress power to prohibit trade with Great Britain, pay American soldiers from Continental funds, and allow impressment of supplies for the army. He was unsuccessful, though, in expanding the power of federal courts or compelling states to redeem Continental currency. Continual dependence on the unanimity of states for national policy, even routine business, continued to frustrate Madison's attempts at "acts necessary for the general good"[21]—"general good" meaning national defense.

By November 1782, Madison had become convinced that the national government's power to tax independent of state control was essential to a successful conduct of the war. His solution was a Congressional tax on imports to the nation, an "impost" that would be exercised by national authority and provide venues for the army, while servicing the debt and funding the federal government.[22] By attaching the military's and creditors' interests to the national regime, Madison saw two powerful constituencies supporting centralized authority and national solvency. A proposed 5 percent levy on imports would allow Congress to gain its own revenues. Twelve state legislatures approved the impost amendment to the Articles of Confederation, but one (Rhode Island) refused; since amendments required unanimous approval, the impost was defeated. Madison fumed at this: in his eyes, the littlest, most insignificant state was damaging the entire national defense effort. "The obstinacy of Rhode Island" he wrote, is "a blow to our credit abroad as well as our future credit at home" (72). This puny state's obstinacy he attributed to the petty motive of jealousy and envy. "If there are not revenue laws which operate at the same time through all the states, and are exempt from the control of each—the mutual jealousies which begin already to appear among them all will assuredly defraud both our foreign and domestic creditors of their just claims" (73).

In 1783 Madison claimed to Edmund Randolph that "Congress are still engaged on the subject of providing adequate revenues for the public debts, particularly that due the army," but the "mutual jealousies among the states" continued to thwart those efforts, while "the discontents and designs of the army are every day taking a more solemn form . . . now whispered that they have not only resolved not to lay down their arms till justice is done them [but] that to prevent surprise a public declaration will be made to that effect" (73–74). In this perilous situation, Madison pondered whether "prosperity and tranquility, or confusion and disunion are to be the fruits of the Revolution." His belief in the reality of human sin and depravity caused Madison to prepare for the worst. Envy and selfishness could easily turn to civil war, anarchy, and foreign intervention. "The consequences of such a situation," he wrote, "would probably be that alliances would be sought first by the weaker and then by the stronger party and this country be made subservient to the wars and politics of Europe" (75). "The wages of sin is death," said St. Paul (Rom. 6:23); Madison saw that warning as applicable to nations as well as individuals.

Ever hopeful and diligent however, in April 1783 Madison drafted a new impost law, one more attractive to a confederacy of autonomous, sovereign states. Collectors of the import tax would be appointed by each state, which would retain the revenues until requisitioned by Congress; the impost would be limited to a period of twenty-five years and could only be used to pay off the principal and interest of the federal debt. Congress passed Madison's plan, and he then wrote an impassioned plea for all the states to accept it. He insisted it was necessary "to render the fruits of the revolution" complete, "a full reward for the blood, the toils, the cares and the calamities which have purchased it." Although the import tax had been devised for repaying the national debt (which was challenged by most states, who suspected corruption and profiteering), Madison argued that it was not a burden attached by "ambition and of vain glory" but a tax "fairly contracted" which "justice and good faith demand . . . should be fully discharged" (76). He reminded the states that the revolution for which these debts were incurred had been fought for "the rights of human nature" and that it was only "by the blessings of the author of these rights" that "they have prevailed." Gratitude to God and fidelity to His values of "justice, good faith, honor, gratitude and all the other qualities which enable the character of a nation" are America's "cardinal and essential virtues" (77–78). Abandonment of moral and financial obligations were an offense against God's providential protection as well as poor national policy.

Yet even this tamer proposal was defeated. As peace prospects improved, states saw even less need for granting revenue authority to the central government. Madison became discouraged and disillusioned over the prospects of an orderly republic given the human foibles of its citizenry. To add injury to insult, in June 1783 a mutiny of soldiers drove Congress out of Philadelphia to Princeton. These political disappointments were then exacerbated by a personal one: Madison's fiancée, Kitty Floyd, broke off their engagement and married a young medical student. Madison wrote to Jefferson with characteristic reserve, saying, "My disappointment has proceeded from several dilatory circumstances on which I had not calculated" (79). Madison's unhappiness over these public and private setbacks was softened by his characteristically low expectations of others and the Christian charity that "hopes all things," which still remained in his mind. To Jefferson he confided: "This picture of our affairs is not a flattering one; but we have been witnesses of so many cases in which evils and errors have been the parents of their own remedy, that we cannot but view it with the consolations of hope" (81). He seemed to come close to quoting that favorite evangelical verse of the Apostle Paul, "all things work together for good to them that love God, to them who are the called according to his purpose" (Rom. 8:28).

An economic depression in 1784, exacerbated by separate states' economic policies, prompted a convention sponsored by Virginia to deal with the regulation of commerce in the nation. Writing to James Monroe on August 7, 1785, Madison indicated he saw the economic problems as directly related to the political inadequacies of the Articles of Confederation: "How are these [trade problem solutions] to be effectuated? Only by harmony in the measures of the states. How is this harmony to be obtained? Only by an acquiescence of all the states in the opinion of a reasonable majority. If Congress as they are now constituted, cannot be trusted with the power of digesting and enforcing this opinion, let them be otherwise constituted" (97). Disunion in foreign trade put the new American states at the mercy of European interests and fomented internal jealousy, strife, and anarchy. "When Massachusetts set on foot a retaliation of the policy of G[reat] B[ritain]," Madison wrote, "Connecticut declared her ports free. New Jersey served New York in the same way Delaware . . . has lately followed the example in opposition to the commercial plans of Pennsylvania. A miscarriage of this attempt to unite the states in some effectual way will have another effect of a serious nature."

That serious effect was a decline of overall import revenue, which, as it had during the war, resulted in inadequate national defense supplies. "The payments from the states under the calls of Congress have in no year borne any proportion to the public wants, another unhappy effect of a continuance of the present anarchy of our commerce" (99). The commercial conference called by Virginia and held in Annapolis in 1786 was attended by only five state delegations, so another convention was called for May 1787 in Philadelphia to "render the constitution of the federal government adequate to the exigencies of the Union" (100). The local rebellion against the state government in Massachusetts known as "Shay's Rebellion," in February 1787, accentuated the dangers of weak central authority in keeping order, adding urgency to the move towards a new constitution. On his way to the Annapolis convention, Madison heard evidence of the deteriorating national condition: "No money comes into the public treasury, trade is on a wretched footing, and the states are running mad after paper money."[23] He summarized the political calamity of the Articles of Convention just prior to the

Constitutional Convention of 1787: "The present system neither has nor deserves advocates . . . no money is paid into the public treasury; no respect is paid to the federal authority. Not a single state complies with the requisitions, several pass them over in silence, and some positively reject them."[24]

Madison's aversion to the "vices" of the American Confederation was reinforced by the "literary cargo" he received from Jefferson in France in 1786—books from Europe describing almost every historical experiment with federated and confederated governments, from ancient Greece to the medieval Holy Roman Empire to modern Swiss, Dutch, and German regimes. From this research, Madison composed the pamphlets "Notes on Ancient and Modern Confederacies" and, later, "Vices of the Political System of the United States." In the former, he concluded that the "regular faults" of historical confederacies were the jealousies and animosities of member states, which a weak central government was inadequate to control: "the jealousy in each province of its sovereignty renders the practice very different from the theory" (i.e., the reality of human selfishness at the state level thwarts the "harmony and virtue" of the ideal Greek polis).[25]

In the "Vices" article, Madison elucidated these historic propensities and how they related to the American colonies' experience. The worst of these vices were: (1) "Failure of the states to comply with the Constitutional requisitions . . . naturally from the number and independent authority of the states"; (2) "Encroachment by the states on the federal authority," which was a constant "temptation" where national coercive authority was absent; (3) "Violations of the laws of nations and of treaties," making consistent foreign policy impossible; (4) "Trespasses of the states on the rights of each other . . . adverse to the spirit of the Union . . . vexatious in themselves . . . [and] destructive of the general harmony" of the Union (using the term *trespasses* for *sins*—common to the Anglican version of the Lord's Prayer); (5) "Want of consent in matters where common interest requires it," such as national defense, currency, trade regulations, naturalization, patents, and internal utilities; (6) Inadequate guards against "internal violence" or illegal rebellion and strife where the single state government is inadequate to suppress the violence of an organized and criminal minority and protect the natural rights (Locke's life, liberty, and property) from invasion; (7) "Want of sanction of the laws" in national statutes without coercive power to enforce them, rendering those federal legislation "nothing more than a treaty of amity . . . between so many independent and sovereign states," tenuous given human weakness and foibles; (8) "Want of ratification" of the central constitution by the people at large, making "a law of a state . . . [that is] repugnant to an act of Congress . . . at least questionable whether the former will must not prevail," causing "insecurity of private rights" to which, given man's propensity to sin when he can get away with it, "neither morality nor religion offered an adequate check."[26]

The reality, in Madison's Augustinian Christian worldview, was that confederate forms of government either promote or accentuate certain human sins: narrow, selfish parochial interests which led to certain definite political consequences like disorganized and inadequate foreign relations of the confederacy (involving defense and commerce) and internal oppression of minorities by majorities, ultimately violating individuals' natural rights to life, liberty, and property. So he addressed these political evils resulting from human nature by focusing on the need for a strong central government to provide effective, unified foreign policy (military and commercial) and to protect individual Lockean rights within the states by means of national constitutional guarantees. "The great desideration in government," he concluded in "The Vices" article, "is such a modification of the Sovereignty as will render it sufficiently neutral between the different interests and factions, to control one part of the society from invading the rights of another, and at the same time sufficiently controlled itself, from setting up an interest adverse to that of the whole society" (106).

Thus, his constitutional system of "checks and balances" assumed evil emanated from individuals, from organized individuals ("factions"), from organized groups controlling politics (states), and from factions attempting to control the central government. His solution, which was proposed in a letter to George Washington in April 1787, just before the Constitutional Convention convened in Philadelphia, and eventually became the Virginia Plan, addressed all these concerns. "Conceiving that an individual independence of the States is utterly irreconcilable with aggregate sovereignty," he wrote, "and that a consolidation of the whole into one simple republic would be as inexpedient as it is unattainable, I have sought for some middle ground, which may at once support a due supremacy at the national authority, and not exclude the local authorities wherever they can be subordinately useful." Madison insisted in his draft of the new constitution that "the national government should be armed with positive and complete authority in all cases which require uniformity; such as the regulation of trade, . . . taxing both exports and imports, the fixing of forms etc." (107, 108). Unified action of a national sort was needed primarily, for Madison, in foreign affairs and internal economic matters.

After the frustrations of the war Congress, Madison wanted "a negative *in all cases whatsoever,* on the legislative acts of the states as . . . absolutely necessary," otherwise, he warned, "states will continue to invade the national jurisdiction, to violate treaties and the law of nations all to harass each other with rival and spiteful measures dictated by mistaken views of interest . . . [and] aggressions of interested majorities on the rights of minorities and of individuals" (108–9). His new constitution would create a "disinterested and passionate [Lockean] umpire in disputes between different passions and interests in the state" emanating from man's sinful nature. Madison then detailed to General Washington the extensive national executive and judicial powers in his plan, concluding that "a government composed of such extensive powers should be well organized and balanced," as well as ratified by "the people" of the nation rather than the states, "to give a new [federal] system its proper validity and energy" (109–10) and eliminate forever the states' obstruction of national prerogatives (including coercion and taxation). With this plan, Madison attended the Constitutional Convention prepared to address the vices of the American polity.

CHAPTER FOUR

LOCKEAN LIBERALISM REALIZED

Construction and Ratification of the U.S. Constitution

The aim of every political constitution is . . . to obtain for
rulers men who possess most wisdom to discern, and most
virtue to pursue, the common good of society, . . . and . . .
to take the most effectual precautions for keeping them vir-
tuous whilst they continue to hold their public trust.
　　　　　　　　　　　　　　　　　—James Madison, 1788

JAMES MADISON had seen the greatest threat from human evil in
American society as the chaos of a headless confederacy and the violations of individual rights by oppressive communities. Therefore
he argued for a national constitution that would provide for a
strong central government capable of protecting individual rights to
life, liberty, and property. The envy and jealousy of state governments promised internal conflict and external foreign domination,
while the egalitarianism and greed of local communities threatened
private property and prosperity. At this time, to Madison, the danger of tyranny from a strong national regime seemed a lesser danger
compared to the immediate threats to America from predatory European countries and selfish factions within the colonies. The threat
of potential national tyranny over states' rights could be addressed
through the structure of constitutional government, but damage
from hostile foreign powers and domestic turmoil could only be
ameliorated through a unified, strong, stable nation. The choice was
never, for Madison, between an imperfect and a perfect govern-

ment; it was always (given human sin and ignorance) between the more or the less imperfect political structures. "I never expect to see a perfect work from imperfect man," it was written in the last *Federalist Paper*, and Madison insisted in *Federalist* #40 that "the choice must always be made, if not of the lesser evil, at least of the GREATER, not the PERFECT good"; and so, "a faultless plan was not to be expected . . . the fallibility to which . . . a body of men [are] liable."[1]

Madison arrived for the Constitutional Convention in Philadelphia on May 3, 1787. He was thirty-six years old. Among his fellow delegates were many of his Continental Congress colleagues from revolutionary days; thirty-nine of the fifty-five delegates had served in Congress and so were well acquainted, as Madison was, with the problems of the Articles of Confederation. Along with the Continental Convention, the city of Philadelphia was hosting at this time two church conventions (Presbyterian and Baptist) and the military aristocracy society of Cincinnati. The Constitutional Convention met six days a week, from late morning to early evening, for four months.[2] Madison was the unofficial chronicler of the convention and chose a seat in the front of the meeting room, in the center, where he could hear every delegate speak. Using a shorthand during the sessions, Madison would write out completely each day's debates within a day or two of having recorded them. This arduous work was motivated by his intellectual interest in the forming of governments, especially confederacies:

> The curiosity I had during my researches into the History of the most distinguished Confederacies, particularly those of antiquity, and the deficiency I found in the means of satisfying it more especially in what related to the process, the principles, the reasons, and the anticipations, which prevailed in the formation of them, determined me to preserve as far as I could an exact account of what might pass in the Convention whilst executing its trust, with the magnitude of which I was duly impressed, as I was with the gratification promised to future curiosity by an authentic exhibition of the new system of Government was to receive its peculiar structure and organization.[3]

Madison the historian was also keenly aware of "the value of such a contribution to the fund of materials for the History of a Constitution on which would be staked the happiness of a people great even in its infancy, and possibly the cause of Liberty throughout the world" (131). The result, *Debates in the Federal Convention*, was not published until fifty years later, when Congress authorized its release in 1840. In it, Madison had recorded all the arguments over every aspect of the U.S. Constitution, as well as the sectional and philosophical sources of those arguments. His own comments at the convention, recorded in the third person, reveal Madison's underlying motives in crafting a constitution that abolished the confusion of the Articles' confederacy and the evils of communitarian tyranny while forming a powerful central government for defense, order, and the protection of individuals' rights to liberty and property. Madison and other delegates were daily reminded of the worst qualities of human nature, as they had to walk past the Walnut Street Prison on their way to the State House and listen to the prisoners shout "foul and horrid imprecations" from the jailhouse windows (135).

The convention began deliberations from the Virginia Plan, heavily indebted to Madison, which provided for a vigorous national government founded on the authority of the *people* (not states), empowered to legislate "in all cases to which the separate states are incompetent," to negate state laws, coerce state governments, and generally to establish "a supreme national government" (133). Madison expressed approval of this scheme for its "providing more effectually for the security of private rights" against "the abuse of it practiced in some of the States" (134). Foreshadowing *Federalist* #10, Madison insisted that the sins of envy and greed would lead to violations of rights where government was not vast enough to control tyrannical majorities. "These observations are verified," he told the Convention, "in the Histories of every Country ancient and modern. In Greece and Rome the rich and poor, the creditors and debtors, as well as patricians and plebeians alternately oppressed each other with equal unmercifulness." The same, he argued, was happening in the states of newly liberated America. "Debtors have defrauded their creditors [e.g., in Rhode Island, through liberal bankruptcy laws]. The landed interest has borne hard on the mercantile interest. The Holders of one species of property have thrown a disproportion of taxes on the holders of another species. The lesson we are to draw from the whole is that where a majority are united by common sentiment, and have an opportunity, the rights of the minor party become insecure" (135).

Madison's familiar pluralist solution quickly follows: "The only remedy is to enlarge the sphere, and thereby divide the community into so great a number of interest and parties, that in the first place a majority will not be likely at the same moment to have a common interest separate from that of the whole or of the minority; and in the second place, that in case they should have such an interest, they may not be apt to unite in the pursuit of it" (135). A large nation, ruled by a strong national government, would for Madison pit evil against evil, sin against sin, "ambition against ambition," among a sufficiently large number of groups that no single one could ever entirely control the state and oppress others.[4] "A republican system on such a scale," he told the convention, "will control all the evils which have been experienced."[5] His Christian realism concerning the nature and persistence of human sin informed this federalist ideology.

Madison's nationalism served his ideal of government as an entity that could protect individual rights against state or community violation. Again, in his view the greatest sin in small localities was the envy of the majority against any minority's wealth, privilege, or other "superior" conditions and the community's attempts to "legally" plunder them. Yet Madison knew the power and influence of the states' leaders and recognized their fear of losing their prerogatives and privilege under a strong central government; so he gradually modified his nationalist language during the convention in order to appease the proud states' rights advocates and state government establishments. He advised the convention to "divide the [public] trust between different bodies of men, who might watch and check each other" because "a people" are "liable to err . . . from fickleness and passion," leading a majority to be "tempted to commit injustice on the minority" (137–38). This danger is especially keen where a majority of the population is poor and "a leveling spirit" incites them to steal the wealth of the prosperous: "An increase of population will necessarily increase the proportion of those who will labor under all the hardships of life, and secretly sigh for a more equal distribution of its blessings. These may outnumber those who are placed above . . . indigence. According to the equal laws of suffrage, the power will slide into the hands of the former" (138). A democracy without constitutional protections of individual rights will soon, out of greed and envy, use the state's power to fleece the rich and satisfy the poor. Stealing from the wealthy is still a sin, Madison believed, even if done under the auspices of law.

This threat of "mobocracy" was most evident at the local and state levels, where poor majorities were concentrated, and indeed the majority rule in such cases led to the abuses of individual rights to property and liberty so prevalent during the Articles of Confederation. Madison told the convention on July 25, 1787, that "the Legislatures of the States had betrayed a strong propensity to a variety of pernicious measures. One object of the National Legislature was to control this propensity" (140). A greater number of prominent, prosperous individuals would make up the national congress, which would check this tendency of poorer local and state governments to fleece the rich. To do so, the federal regime must have the power to negate state statutes "where the law aggrieves individuals." This "serious evil" of state laws violating individual natural rights required, for Madison, "a Constitutional negative on the laws of the states . . . to secure individuals against encroachments on their rights." He found "the injustice of them so frequent and so flagrant as to alarm the most steadfast friends of Republicanism" (147). This Madison wrote in October 1787 to Jefferson, who was much more sanguine about the wisdom and virtue of average citizens in respecting individual, Lockean rights.[6]

For Calvinist Madison, however, the human sins of greed and envy were not easily ameliorated by public education, political participation, or even rough economic equality; and so a strong national government that would have the authority of abolishing state laws that harmed private rights, even to the point of military force, was necessary.[7] "The great desideratum in Government is so to modify the sovereignty as that it may be sufficiently neutral between different parts of the Society to control one part from invading the rights of another, and at the same time sufficiently controlled itself, from setting up an interest adverse to that of the entire Society." Using Locke's image of government as an umpire balancing interests, Madison claimed a dominant national regime would "hold a pretty even balance between the parties of particular states."[8]

Recognizing the fear state leaders had of such national supremacy, Madison moderated his attacks on their "incompetence" and emphasized the central government's authority over and on behalf of *individual* citizens rather than over states' governments.[9] Similarly, he tried to assuage the smaller states' opposition to the strong national government by appealing to their fear of larger states' power, arguing that only a healthy central authority could protect them from the "ambition and power of their larger neighbors" (207). Still, probably remembering Rhode Island's irresponsible conduct during the Revolutionary War, Madison questioned the fairness of the "Great Compromise," which enlisted smaller states' support of the constitution by giving them equal representation in the United States Senate. And while he argued for the popular election of the lower House of Congress—respecting common consent and control by the people—he resisted lowering the percentage to override a presidential veto from three-quarters of the legislature to two-thirds, revealing a continued suspicion of popular impulse (200, 226). A strong executive, he felt, would check mass hysteria, and a strong federal regime would protect individual rights. He even proposed empowering Congress to build canals and other internal improvements, an idea most states resisted, and ensured that creditors would be guaranteed repayment and protection from inflation, through provisions for federal currency and bankruptcy law (226–69). As biographer Ralph Ketcham summarizes it, Madison's mixed, balanced constitution was based on an "assessment of human nature so sober that it found unsafe not governments representing many factions (which could counteract each other), but authoritarian ones, where a greedy, unchecked minority could oppress everyone else" (201).

Madison had guided the new constitution through the many competing interests and factions in the convention and succeeded in reaching a miraculous compromise. During a particularly acrimonious impasse at the convention, Dr. Benjamin Franklin made a plea that sessions be opened with prayer, affirming that "God governs in the affairs of men," but delegates, fearing that a sudden dispatching of clergymen to the hall would alarm the public, declined

Franklin's offer (209). Tempers cooled afterwards, however, and the Constitutional Convention resumed its business smoothly, causing Madison later to exclaim that "it is impossible to consider the degree of concord which ultimately prevailed as less than a miracle."[10]

Madison wrote the cover letter conveying the newly written constitution to the Continental Congress, claiming that the government it created would ensure the "Union . . . prosperity, felicity, [and] perhaps our national existence."[11] In his letter describing the new constitution to Jefferson, Madison summarized its benefits as "(1) to unite a proper energy in the Executive and a proper stability in the Legislative [branches] . . . with the essential characters of Republican Government. (2) To draw a line of demarcation which would give to the Central Government every power requisite for general purposes, and leave to the States every power which might be most beneficially administered by them. (3) To provide for the different interests of different parts of the Union. (4) To adjust the clashing pretensions of the large and small States."[12] He was soon to find that the real battle with the evils of greed and envy, provincial conflicts, and denial of individual rights was just beginning—as the struggle over ratifying the constitution commenced.

RATIFICATION

Madison went from Philadelphia's Constitutional Convention to New York's constitutional ratification battle, stopping in Princeton along the way to pick up an honorary Doctor of Law degree. President Witherspoon conferred the honor, saying that "all concerned in this college were, not barely willing, but proud . . . [to honor] one of their own sons who had done them so much honor by his public service."[13]

In New York, as in Philadelphia, Madison found himself at the center of the intellectual debates over state ratification of the new constitution, and he soon became the acknowledged leader in persuading states to accept the new government. With Gouveneur Morris, John Jay, Robert Livingston, and, especially, Alexander Hamilton, from New York Madison coordinated federalist activity in the various states, served as a clearinghouse for information, and orchestrated responses to antifederalist opposition to the constitution

(232). New York was the "headquarters" of the ratification struggle, and Madison was its leading strategist. News that leaders like George Mason, Patrick Henry, and R. H. Lee in Virginia were opposing the document, that the popular Samuel Adams and prestigious John Hancock were expressing doubts, impressed Madison with how formidable the task of persuading states to accept the constitution would be. He found such a prominent league of opponents "melancholy proof of the fallibility of the human judgement," falling back on his Calvinist view of the human capacity for self-deception. He recognized that many of the most distinguished antifederalists had been schooled in the state governments and simply saw no need for a stronger central government (237). Despite their parochial views, Madison still held that most citizens were tired of "the vicissitudes, injustice, and follies" of the headless monster of confederacy and were "impatient for some change which promises stability and repose" from foreign intervention and communities' violation of individual rights (238).

By the autumn of 1787, the opponents of the new constitution were rallying so successfully that believers in the new American government urged Madison, Hamilton, and Jay to write a definitive defense of the new structure, advocating its advantages and defeating opponents' attacks upon it. The result, eight-five *Federalist Papers*, began to be published in New York newspapers and soon was being circulated among all the states, becoming what Ketcham calls "the authoritative commentary on the Constitution and the best-known work of political theory ever written in the United States" (239). Madison's contributions (nos. 10, 14, 18–20, 37–58, and 62–63) reflect not only the arguments for a federal republic made during the Constitutional Convention but also his underlying Christian outlook on the nature of man and society. Many scholars have noted that the *Federalist Papers* were written as political propaganda to persuade state ratifying conventions to approve the new constitution and therefore cleverly concealed the most provocative elements to staunch antifederalists, but Madison's pieces show a remarkable honesty and forthrightness in criticizing the states' autonomy under the Articles of Confederation. While not totally dismissing the potential threat of a strong national government becoming tyrannical in the future, they consistently subordinate that threat to the more immediate and dangerous realities of foreign domination of disparate states, factious conflicts, and local oppression of individual natural rights.

MADISON'S *FEDERALIST PAPERS*

In his first and most famous *Federalist Paper*, #10, Madison identifies the advantage of the constitutional union to "break and control the violence of faction," which he calls the "mortal disease" of popular governments.[14] He defines *faction* as "a number of citizens, whether . . . a majority or minority of the whole, who are united and actuated by some common impulse of passion, or of interest, adverse to the rights of other citizens, or to the permanent and aggregate interests of the community" (123). It might be an economic faction like farmers or banks; it might be a religious faction like Catholics or Protestants; or it might be a regional faction like Northerners or Southerners. Today it might be a particular industry or movement such as tobacco or environmental groups; miners or women; Buddhists or the gay rights lobby. The source of all these potentially oppressive factions is the same for Madison: "self-love," ambition, sin, each human's desire to have his or her own way, be the center of the universe, impose his or her agenda or interests on everyone—in short, humans' desire for domination. "The latest causes of faction," Madison insists, "are sown in the nature of man." This Augustinian Christian view of humanity as willful and selfish, proud and arrogant, led Madison to conclude that individual ambition for preeminence and power among all humans would lead to them to use politics to "vex and oppress each other." This "propensity of mankind" towards "mutual animosities" will show itself in "the most frivolous and fanciful distinctions," causing jealousy, resentment, and anger "sufficient to kindle their unfriendly passions and excite their most violent conflicts" (124).

Wherever people come together, they will end up fighting—ostensibly over policies and principles but actually over wounded pride and desire for attention, glory, and adulation; and fierce resentment will brew when each does not get his or her own way. One thinks of St. Paul saying that the fruit of this sinful nature are "hatred, discord, jealousy . . . selfish ambition, dissensions, factions," and so on (Gal. 5:20). Not everyone, for Madison, is freed by Christ from these natural lusts, so religion alone cannot be relied upon to curb them. The reality for him is that human vices will take their worst form in political oppression, and therefore a political remedy must be found to combat them. That remedy is the constitutional federation, which divides power and pits ambition against ambition, thwarting any individual's or group's evil intents from ever dominating. The cause of factions cannot be removed, but their effects can be controlled with the right structure of government (125). Different natural faculties, gifts, and talents in individuals give rise, Madison explained, to different economic and occupational abilities and benefits. The resulting differences in property ownership and financial positions are "the most common and durable source of factions." From different economic conditions come conflicting interests (creditors vs. debtors; agrarian vs. urban; commerce vs. industrial), which strive to form factions and parties to advance their interests in the government. "The protection of these faculties" and the property that results from them "is the first object of government," wrote Madison, echoing Locke (124). So "the great object" of political society is how to secure the public good while protecting the property rights of the individuals composing it.

A pure, classical democracy cannot cure the "mischiefs of faction" Madison argued, because such direct democracies have "ever been spectacles of turbulence and contention . . . incompatible with personal security or the rights of property" (125). A constitutional republic, however, has a greater chance of addressing the problem by delegating government to a smaller group of representations who are of higher character than average citizens and extending the sphere of governance over a larger area, encompassing a larger number of factions and thereby diminishing the relative power of each. This will "enlarge and refine the public views by passing them through the medium of a chosen body of citizens, whose wisdom may best discern the true interest of their country and whose patriotism and love of justice will be least likely to sacrifice it to temporary or partial considerations." In other words, those elected to national government will more likely be the "elect" of God in the Calvinist sense—those whose Christian experience has shown them the truth of Scripture and the reality of human sin, greed, and lust for power, and who are humble in the use of political authority, serving God and the public good as a divine "calling"—diminishing the ferocity of factional conflict. A more extensive republic is the "most favorable to the election of proper guardians of the public weal . . . [because] if the proportion of fit characters be not less in the larger than in the small republic, the former will present a greater option [or larger pool of capable leaders] and consequently a greater probability of a fit choice" (126).

Madison does not explain how a factious population is likely to select these men of superior moral character over narrow, selfish individuals like themselves or why the "elect" in the Godly sense will desired to be "elected" in the worldly sense. He simply states that given the small number of genuine, God-fearing Christians, a larger political field from which to choose is necessary to get enough in government to pursue the public good. Even while not fully explaining this benefit of the new constitutional system, though, Madison insists that enlarging the sphere for factional activity diminishes the dangers of any one gaining enough political power to oppress everyone else. "The greater the number of citizens and extent of territory . . . renders factious combinations less dreaded. . . . Extend the sphere and you take in greater variety of parties and interests; you make it less probable that a majority of the whole will have a common motive to invade the rights of other citizens . . . more difficult for all who feel it to discover their own strength and to act in unison with each other" (127). In short, he calls for American pluralism: many parties and interest groups balancing each other, allowing the superior leaders with "enlightened views and virtuous sentiments" to be above "local prejudices and . . . schemes of injustice," securing the individual rights of all. Such pernicious schemes—a single state church, abolition of debts, equal division of property, or "any other improper or wicked project"—are less likely to occur in a large constitution republic than in a small community or state (128). Madness is diluted in larger seas.

The multiplication of interests over a large territory and the subsequent weakening of each in its power to oppress others is clearly explained by Madison in *Federalist* #10 and gives strength to his arguments for ratifying the constitution. His promise that ignoble masses would elect noble representatives and that the noble would want to go into public service is more problematical. Of course, Calvin, as Madison knew, maintained that government service or "magistracy" is the highest divine calling—equal to the ordained ministry itself. It seemed this, for Madison, would provide sufficient incentive for decent, able individuals to go into public service —out of a sense of duty and service.[15] Perhaps he thought by a similar "grace of God" common sinners would then elect them to office.

In his next paper, *Federalist* #14, Madison repeats the distinction between a republican (representative) and a democratic (direct) form of government and reassures states that the national power under the new constitution would be limited to "enumerated objects which will not interfere with their sovereignty," as the state governments retain "due authority and activity" over all "other objects" (141–43). Madison, ironically, lists internal improvement of roads and canals, which some antifederalists did not consider one of the constitutional prerogatives of the central regime, along with defense of the Western frontier, as premier federal obligations. Still, he urges a "manly spirit" in resisting the "gloomy" opponents of union, whose "fashionable" but "unnatural voice" claims that the American people "knit together . . . by so many cords of affection" cannot live together as members of the "same family." Rather, Madison insists, "the mingled blood which they have shed in defense of their sacred rights" can easily draw them together into "public happiness" (144).

Madison's *Federalist* #18, #19, and #20 draw upon his research into historical confederacies, which corroborates the disastrous war experience of America under the Articles of Confederation. The ancient Greek confederacy, Madison finds, was wracked by "domestic vicissitudes, convulsions and carnage" finally resulting in its destruction. "Mutual jealousies, fears, hatreds and injuries" characterized ancient Greece, just as modern America, and its confederacies' "weakness and disorders" finally ended in the ruin and slavery of the Athenians, as would happen for the Americans if a new constitution was not adopted (#18, 160–61). In more recent history, Madison cites the German confederacy as a good example of the disastrous effects of weak central government. Germany reveals that a community of sovereigns "renders the empire a nerveless body incapable of regulating its own members, insecure against external dangers, and agitated with unceasing fermentations in its own bowels"; besides such political indigestion, Madison presents the modern German confederacy as also characterized by "general imbecility, confusion and misery." Comparing this country's experience with the Polish and Swiss confederacies, Madison finds all displaying "jealousies, pride [and] clashing pretensions," revealing all "the deformities of [a] political monster"—specifically, a headless monster (#19, 165–66). Such is the fate of America, if it does not reform its confederacy.

In his examination of the Dutch confederacy of republics (the "United Netherlands"), Madison discusses in *Federalist* #20 a similar modern tale of woe: domestic discord, foreign interference, and another "melancholy . . . lesson of history"; tyranny flows from weak government. It is better, history teaches, to "establish [a] union and render it the parent of tranquility, freedom and happiness" (#20, 170–72). For Madison, the antifederalists, who favored states' rights, failed to see the threat of anarchy and destruction in loose confederations; they neglected to realize that the choice is not between absolute freedom and merciless tyranny but between ordered authority and tyranny. The former, by substituting "the mild and salutary *coercion* of the *magistracy*" for the inevitable *violence* in confederacies, leads to gratitude mingled with "an ejaculation to Heaven for the propitious concord" replacing "selfish passions" (172). The visionary antifederalists (or, today, classical republican communitarians) failed to recognize that "tyranny has perhaps oftener grown out of the assumptions of power called for, by a defective constitution, than out of the full exercise of the largest constitutional authority" (171). Again, the greatest threat to American liberty at this point in its history was not an overbearing central government but the chaos of independent state sovereignties and European interference with, and manipulation of, the resulting anarchy.

In *Federalist* #37 Madison begins a systematic defense of the specific provisions of the constitution, beginning with a reply to its opponents' charges that it would establish a centralized tyranny. "It is a misfortune, inseparable from *human affairs*," (i.e., sin), Madison proclaims, "that public measures are rarely investigated with that spirit of moderation which is essential to a just estimate of their real tendency to advance or obstruct the public good." That is, for Madison, it is a pity that not all Americans are as calm, rational, experienced, and well-educated as he is; and so they are prone to display their human weaknesses and sin so profligately. While not wishing to "insinuate . . . the purity of their intentions," Madison finds the "many passions and interest" opposing the new constitution and many "dispositions unfriendly" to its provisions a bit disappointing. These opponents "magnify the faults" of the document when, in fairness, "a faultless plan was not to be expected" given the fallibility of mortal, sinful, men. Madison recommends Christian humility to these critics of the constitution and its framers, advising them to "keep in mind that they themselves also are but men and ought not to assume an infallibility in prejudging the fallible opinions of others" (#37, 242)—a neat paraphrase of Jesus' admonition in The Sermon on the Mount: "Judge not, less ye be judged" (Matt. 7:1). This may sound snide or even hypocritical to our twenty-first-century ears, but it undoubtedly resonated in many eighteenth-century minds schooled in the Bible and Christian principles as a valuable reminder of human evil's tendency to come out as purported virtue, or self-righteousness.

Madison asks for understanding of the enormous challenges of revising the American government, acknowledging that the "difficulties [are] inherent in the very nature of the undertaking." The major difficulty in any such plan of government, Madison argues, is somehow combining the "requisite stability and energy in government with the inviolable attention due to liberty and to the republican form," balancing freedom and order. Unlike the visionary, optimistic antifederalists, who believed a decentralized classical republic would foster public virtue and social harmony, Madison's Calvinism found stability over unruly human nature by a strong government "among the chief blessings of civil society." Yet it doesn't happen automatically. Natural man's tendency is towards evil, violence, and oppression. Keeping that nature in check is an essential element of good government. "The genius of *republican* liberty," for Madison, "seems to demand on one side not only that all power should be derived from the people, but that those intrusted with it should be kept in dependence on the people by a short duration of their appointments" (243). It was that "arduous" task of "marking the

proper line" between liberty and authority, state sovereignty and national power, that the writers of the constitution had to tackle, and
Madison advises that their opponents ought to be a bit more sym-
pathetic to these difficulties and not so quick to criticize and judge.
Given "the imperfections of human faculties" and "the experience
of ages," which shows that social relations will ever "puzzle the
greatest adepts in political science," Madison urges his contempo-
raries to moderate "still further our expectations and hopes from
the efforts of human sagacity." Yet he knows that such important issues will always remain "a pregnant source of ingenious disquisition
and controversy" (244).

Again begging his opponents to have patience and humility,
Madison points out that even Holy Scripture is not perfectly clear,
on account of foggy human minds: "When the Almighty himself
condescends to address mankind in their own language, his meaning, luminous as it must be, is rendered dim and doubtful by the
cloudy medium through which it is communicated"—that is, the
human mind. Not trying to suggest that the framers are Godlike,
their constitution like Holy Writ, or its critics of clouded mind,
Madison only implies that they should study it more carefully before dismissing it unjustly. He suggests three sources of "vague and
incorrect definitions" or "comprehensions": (1) indistinctness of the
object or constitutional provision; (2) imperfections of the organ
of conception (the brain); and (3) inadequateness of the vehicle of
ideas, or language conveying the meaning (245). Any of these can
lead to misunderstandings of the new constitution, according to
Doctor Madison.

Given the Constitutional Convention's task of delineating the
proper boundaries between national and state jurisdictions within a
federal republic, it was subject to all three of these sources of confusion. The miracle, to Madison, was that so many of the difficulties
involved were surmounted by a group of disparate, fallible men,
with unprecedented unanimity. "It is impossible for the man of
pious reflection not to perceive in it a finger of that Almighty hand
which has been so frequently and signally extended to our relief in
the critical stages of the revolution" (245, 246). Only the favor and
blessing of God can explain it, not human wisdom or goodness.

Addressing the constitution's opponents in *Federalist* #38, Madi-

son compares them, and America under the Articles of Confederation, to a medical patient whose illness grows worse daily but,
when the physician prescribes a remedy, first denies the sickness and
then accuses the doctor of prescribing poison. Madison insists the
symptoms of America's malady are everywhere to be seen (sectional
conflict, foreign intervention, poor circulation of money), but the
antifederalists ignore them and then expect any improvement in
their condition to come without any side-effects or imperfections
(249, 252). Upon treatment, they sue the doctor for malpractice.

In *Federalist* #39, Madison again defines the new constitution as
establishing a "republic"—by which he means a form of government
like those in Holland, Venice, Poland, and England, in which the
government is administered by representatives of the people and
"by persons holding their offices during pleasure for a limited period, or during good behavior." He goes on to point out that the
House of Representatives is elected directly by the whole people,
the U.S. Senate indirectly from the people, the president indirectly
from the people, and the judiciary for tenure during good behavior
(255). The fear of a strong president is addressed by the constitutional impeachment clause, and the constitution's republican quality
is affirmed by its "absolute prohibition of titles of nobility and its
ratification by deputies elected by the people." Madison points
out that antifederalist concerns over its centralized authority arise
from the failure to see that the constitution is a blend of national
and federal:

> In requiring more than a majority, and particularly in comput-
> ing the proportion by the *States,* not by *citizens,* it departs from
> the national and advances to the *federal* character; in rendering
> the concurrence of less than the whole number of States suffi-
> cient, it loses again the federal and partakes of the *national* char-
> acter. . . . In its foundation it is federal, not national, in the
> sources from which the ordinary powers of the government are
> drawn, it is partly federal and partly national; in the operation
> of these powers, it is national, not federal; in the extent of them,
> again, it is federal, not national; and finally, in the authoritative
> mode of introducing amendments, it is neither wholly federal
> nor wholly national. (259)

One begins to see why few delegates wanted to argue with James Madison. Of course in this paper, as in others, he is using "federal" as opposed to "national" to denote the area of governance shared by state and national sovereignties, attempting to reassure states' rights advocates that the new constitution reserved many powers for the decentralized authorities.

In *Federalist* #40 Madison continues this tack, insisting that the new document is merely an "expansion of principles" of the Articles of Confederation and not truly original or radically different. The convention merely "corrected" the "errors" of the earlier political structure (263). In every social system, "a power to advance the public happiness involves a discretion which may be misapplied and abused"; but, Madison repeats in *Federalist* #41, "the purist of human blessings must have a portion of alloy in them" and "the choice must always be made, if not of the lesser evil, at least of the GREATER, not the PERFECT good" (266). The important advantages of the new constitution over the former Articles of Confederation are: (1) security against foreign danger; (2) regulation of intercourse with foreign nations; (3) maintenance of harmony and proper intercourse among the states; (4) "certain miscellaneous objects of general utility"; (5) restraint of the states from certain injurious acts; (6) "provisions for giving due efficacy to all these powers." Of course, items (4) and (6) are precisely those the antifederalists feared would lead to national tyranny. But Madison goes on to enumerate these specific, limited constitutional powers of the national regime, which should assuage those fears. They include declaring war, granting letters of marque, providing for armies and navy fleets, regulating militia, and levying and borrowing money.

The necessity of such services in a nation seem axiomatic to Madison; at any rate, he suggests that his answer to objections to these powers "seems to be so obvious and conclusive as scarcely to justify such a discussion in any place"—an old debate trick of rejecting opponents without confronting their true arguments (267). As for the objection to a national standing army, which classical republicans in favor of states' rights fear as preliminary to national tyranny, Madison removes such opposition with reference to the limited term (two years) of military revenues voted by the most popular branch of the national government, the House of Representatives (268–69). Madison addresses the "miscellaneous powers" in *Federalist* #43, finding patent and copyright law, if not essential to the central regime, nevertheless useful in promoting "the public good" (279). Madison defends provisions guaranteeing states a republican form of government (against potential monarchical or aristocratic regimes) and protecting against the domestic violence of criminal gangs (e.g., Shay's Rebellion) as obvious benefits of the constitution, despite the exaggerated claims of antifederalist opponents (281–82). The national power to repay foreign debts, which many states' rights advocates also construed as potentially tyrannical, Madison dismisses with the belief that debts fairly contracted are a moral obligation, criticizing the "pretended" doctrine that the successful conclusion of the Revolutionary War "has the magical affect of dissolving its moral obligation." The constitution's amendment procedure is defended by Madison as striking a happy medium between a too mutable foundation and one whose "discovered faults" are impossible to alter. That states can initiate such amendments to the constitution should allay many fears of states' rights advocates, he maintains (284).

Similarly, in *Federalist* #44, Madison tries to reassure the states that the constitutional restrictions on their authority are reasonable and in their best interest. Provisions giving the national government exclusive power over treaties and coinage, as well as those against state laws impairing the obligations of contracts, simply recognized that these activities were best accomplished across state boundaries and jurisdictions, that is, they are truly national in character. The constitutional grant of authority to the central government to accomplish their appropriate duties was simply a logical extension of those national purposes. The provision to "make all laws which shall be necessary and proper for carrying into execution of the foregoing powers" is simply an extension of the central government's responsibilities; without which, Madison argues, "the whole Constitution would be dead letters." One cannot expect a ruler to assume responsibility without granting him the authority necessary to do so. Rather, "wherever the end is required, the means are authorized," so as not to "disarm the government of all real authority" (288–89). It seemed to Madison that the critics of this constitution wanted the benefits of a national government (security, order, and prosperity) without giving it the power necessary to attain those benefits. These constitutional conditions of effective national government, including the Supremacy Clause, are required to abolish the "impotent condition" of the Articles of Confederation (291).

The next two papers, *Federalist* #45 and #46, continue Madison's discussion of the federal nature of the new constitution. He tries to calm the states' fears of centralized tyranny by insisting that "the powers delegated by the proposed Constitution to the federal government are few and defined. These which are to remain in the State governments are numerous and indefinite." Furthermore, Madison notes, those aspects of the national power are primarily international, while the states retain the domestic policy issues dearest to them: "The former will be exercised principally on external objects, as war, peace, negotiations and foreign commerce. . . . The powers reserved to the several states will extend to all the objects, which, in the ordinary course of affairs, concern the lives, liberties and properties of the people, and the internal order, improvement and the prosperity of the State" (#4, 296). In this division of national versus states' sovereignty, the former over external and foreign matters (war, trade, diplomacy) and the latter over internal and domestic policy (education, economics, welfare, courts), Madison agrees with Jefferson's assessment of the right relations between central and decentralized governments.[16]

Madison adds that it is ridiculous for anyone to fear the authority of the federal government, since it will always have far fewer employees than any state will have: "The number of individuals employed under the Constitution of the United States will be much smaller than the number employed under the particular states" (#4, 295). Furthermore, both national and state regimes are "dependent on the great body of the citizens of the United States" (297). They are but "different agents and trustees of the people, constituted with different powers and designed for different purposes," not rivals. The opponents of the federal republic, he continues, have "lost sight of the people" and have therefore "viewed these different establishments not only as mutual rivals and enemies, but as uncontrolled by any common superior," forgetting that "the ultimate authority . . . resides in the people" (297). Besides, Madison assures, the local and state regimes, with their "ties of personal acquaintance and friendship," are the first and natural attachment of people. In the highly unlikely event that future Americans became more attached to and identified with the central government, it could only be because of "such manifest and irresistible proofs of a better administration" of the federal government (297–98). It was much more likely, in Madison's opinion, that the national government would suffer encroachments from the "inflamed zeal" of the state officials (300). In every contest of authority, "the State governments must clearly have the advantage," so the federal government will always be "disinclined to invade the rights of the individual states" (299). The powers of the national government over domestic affairs are far less formidable than those of the state governments (302). Madison's fallibility is evident here, but it should be noted that he died before the Civil War.

In the next seven papers, Madison discusses how the separation of powers within the national government further guarantees the states' sovereignty and protection from centralized tyranny. The accumulation of political power in the same hands (or branch of government) is, for Madison, "the very definition of tyranny," and he saw the constitution's distribution of power between three distinct branches (executive, legislative, and judicial), in conformance with Baron de Montesquieu's "science of politics," as a just remedy to limiting the strength of the central regime (#47, 302–3). In this sense, the British Constitution, at least before its corruption, is a model for America's—a "mirror of political liberty" for Madison. In that British model, furthermore, those branches are not totally separate but interdependent, checking one another's tyrannical tendencies (303). For example, Madison notes, like the similarly overlapping government branches in the state constitutions of New York, New Jersey, Pennsylvania, Delaware, Maryland, Virginia, North Carolina, South Carolina, and Georgia, the federal structure grants the executive a part in legislation and allows the legislative a judicial function (impeachment), allowing each to police the other's conduct (304). Such "blending" of functions, for Madison, is "essential to a free government." Like the mystery of the Holy Trinity, in which God is at once one and three, Madison believes the proper ordering of government involves the power of one department never being "directly and completely" administered by other departments, but each having an "overlapping influence" on the others (#48, 308). Overall, government power in the new constitution is "divided and balanced" so each branch can be "effectually checked and restrained by the others" (311).

In his most famous phrase, Madison insists in *Federalist* #51 that these checks and balances require that "ambition must be made to counteract ambition." This is merely a "reflection on human nature" (319); the reality of human sin—selfishness, greed, lust for power and domination—allows no other remedy. A few "elect" Christians will view their evil hearts honestly, repent of their sins, and lead humble, relatively benevolent lives; but the majority of humanity, Madison surmises, will remain prone to evil, refuse to acknowledge and repent of it, and tell lies to cover it up, requiring structures pitting evil against evil to minimize its oppressive, destructive tendencies. As the eldest child in a large family, "Jemmy" had ample opportunity to see displays of human selfishness and domination in young children, and this exposure continued in his adult encounters with other politicians. "If men were angels, no government would be necessary," Madison proclaims in *Federalist* #51; "If angels were to govern men, neither external nor internal controls on government would be necessary" (319). But men are men: fallen, selfish, greedy, prideful, and more than happy to use state power to advance personal agendas. They are insulted when it is suggested that their ostensible noble motives mask ambition and arrogance, and they are intolerant of others; essentially, they are evil. Hence, hope for just government lay only in "this policy of supplying, by opposite and rival interests, the defect of better motives, [which] might be traced through the whole system of human affairs, private as well as public." Only then can "the private interest of every individual . . . be a sentinel over the public rights" (320).

So the most just regime comes out of a view of man's greatest injustice; the fairest out of a realization and admission of human unfairness. Any compromise with this strict Augustinian pessimism over unredeemed humanity, any classical republican, enlightenment, communitarian, socialist, or new age optimism that seeks to build a society and government on man's "higher," noble instincts, his virtue or "inner" altruism or spirituality, is doomed not just to failure but to a cruel, hypocritical failure in which the greatest atrocities are committed in the name of the highest ideals. Better to be cautious, prudent, careful; better not to get one's hopes up too high where humans are concerned. Expect the worst, so as not to be deceived as well as disappointed. This is what Niebuhr later called "Christian Realism." For Madison, this means that "security of civil rights must be the same as that for religious rights. It consists in the one case in the multiplicity of interests, and in the other in the multiplicity of sects" (321).

Specific provisions in the new constitution acknowledge this evil interest in the human heart and its propensity to oppress others, even with the noblest of intentions. Biennial elections of Congressional representatives confirms the principle that "the greater the power is, the shorter ought to be its duration" (326). In the powerful House of Representatives, where most "popular" damage can be accomplished, Madison concludes that two years is "the period within which human virtue can bear the temptations of power" (327). Still, republican government assumes more public virtue (enough for self-government) than many other forms of government, such as monarchy or aristocracy. "As there is a degree of depravity in mankind which requires a certain degree of circumspection and distrust," the Calvinist Madison declares in *Federalist* #55, "so there are other qualities in human nature which justify a certain portion of esteem and confidence" (339, 344). He refers to a natural conscience or moral sense; a possible redemption through Christ leading to repentance of sin and humble, unselfish conduct; a gratitude to God for His mercy and grace, prompting a life of duty and service. "Republican government," Madison insists, "presupposes the existence of these qualities in a higher degree than any other form" of government (339). Even in a republican form of government premised on human's capacity for self-governance, however, that confidence in sufficient virtue must be tempered with a Christian sense of mankind's sin and evil, even in believers.

This is partially why Madison gives credit to Britain for many of the lessons and examples, good and bad, employed by the founders in designing the U.S. Constitution. England has given "so many political lessons, both of the monitory and exemplary kind, and which has been frequently consulted in the course of these inquires" (342). Great Britain's historical examples of both noble and ignoble politics provides the underlying principle of Madisonian democracy, that "the aim of every political constitution is . . . to obtain for rulers men who possess most wisdom to discern and most virtue to pursue, the common good of society . . . and . . . to take the most effectual precautions for keeping them virtuous while they continue to hold their public trust" (343). The constitution's popular election of leaders, staggering of terms, distribution of powers amongst different branches and levels of federalism, checks and balances, and policy for orderly amendment does this, in Madison's view. It is not perfect, but perfection is not possible amongst imperfect humanity.

The bicameral legislature provides both responsiveness and stability. The lower House is elected popularly for terms of short duration. This most democratic element of national government forces representatives to be responsive to the people's will to further their own ambition, for they will be unable to make a law "which will not have its full operation on themselves and their friends." The "duty, gratitude, interest, ambition itself, are the cords by which they will be bound to fidelity and sympathy with the great mass of the people" (though even here Madison admits that "these may all be insufficient to control the caprice and wickedness of men" [345]). The upper House, or Senate, however, will add a maturity and "firmness" of aristocracy to Congress, tempering popular passion with the calm judgement of established, wealthy, prominent men. For "it will be of little avail to the people that the laws are made by men of their own choice if the laws be so voluminous that they cannot be read, or so incoherent that they cannot be understood." Frequent popular uproars and changes, to which a childlike, "calamitous" populace is prone, can "poison the blessings of liberty" and require stable, mature judgement to provide balance. If our nation's laws "be repealed or revised before they are promulgated, or undergo such incessant changes that no man who knows what the law is today can guess what it will be tomorrow," it is like having no law. Such vicissitudes further lead to a "diminution of attachment and reverence" to the republican political system and, as in Plato's *Republic*, can open the door to tyranny (368).[17] Hence the advantage of America's republic, in which the people are excluded from government in "their collective capacity" through representation, for "liberty may be endangered by the abuses of liberty as by the abuses of power."[18] On that note, Madison ended his contribution to the *Federalist Papers* and returned to Virginia to fight for his state's ratification of the new constitution.

In another of the many historical ironies surrounding Madison's life at this time, he was elected from his county to the Virginia state constitutional ratifying convention over his rival of eleven years earlier, the tavern keeper Charles Porter, who had poured out free liquor to his constituents. This reversal caused Madison's friends to declare that "the sinners of Orange [County]" have turned "from their wicked ways." Support from the fiery Baptist preacher and second Great Awakening revivalist John Leland didn't hurt Madison either. Meanwhile, Madison arranged for distribution of the new book edition of the *Federalist Papers* for all the convention delegates.[19]

In the Virginia ratifying convention, Madison faced the formidable antifederalist opposition of many prominent patriots, particularly the eloquent and emotional Patrick Henry (257–65). Henry played on old revolutionary fears of tyrannical centralized government and corrupt "British" finances. The classical republican warnings of powerful national government combining with wealthy, corrupt aristocrats to oppress local democracy and virtuous, simple farmers, reverberated in Henry's emotional charges against the new constitution. Wild accusations that Madison's document would abolish the state governments, ruin the sturdy yeoman farmer class, build an enormous standing army, and raise exorbitant federal taxes forced the proconstitution advocates to address each article of the new document. Madison pleaded for examination of the constitution "on its own merits solely," because "giving opinions, and making assertions, will condescend to prove and demonstrate, by fair and regular discussion" the truth of the value of federal government (256). Against Henry's charge that the constitution "endangered the public liberty," Madison explained that it actually protected public liberty better than the old Articles of Confederation, which had overlooked the possibility of "the majority trampling on the rights of the minority," producing "factions and commotions, which, in republics, have more frequently than any other cause, produced despotism." By this constitution, "powers are not given to any particular set of men, they are in the hands of the people" (257).

Under the Articles, the people had been frustrated at a particularly dangerous time (during war) by "a trifling minority" (i.e., Rhode Island). Therefore it was clear that unified national government was necessary to protect America from hostile foreign powers. Furthermore, a strong military was imperative to protect land claims in the Western territories, which many Virginians held (258). Madison defended the central government's direct taxing power as necessary, safe, and economical, and he assured the Virginia convention that Thomas Jefferson (then ambassador to France) would support it "because it enables the government to carry on its operations." Not averse to name-dropping for a good cause, Madison reminded the Virginia Convention delegates that the revered General George Washington also favored ratification of the new constitution (259). He argued that the new national government did not threaten the fundamental rights of individuals or domestic governance by states because its powers were strictly defined and enumerated (262). The horrible prospects of tyranny and oppression portrayed by Henry and his antifederalist brethren could only occur, Madison explained, if there were extreme abuse of those powers by federal officials, and the people reserved the right to vote them out of office in those cases (261). Patrick Henry's extravagant fears bordered on paranoia, and, taken to their logical conclusion, Madison claimed, they would render all government impossible (260).

Henry was really more of an anarchist, hating all and any authority, even legitimate, responsible authority. During one debate, a violent thunderstorm erupted outside as Patrick Henry held forth in dramatic eloquence. A witness wrote: "a storm suddenly arose. It grew dark. The doors came to with a rebound like a peal of musketry. The windows rattled; the huge wooden structure rocked . . . Henry [seemed to have] seized upon the artillery of Heaven, and directed its fiercest thunders against the heads of his adversaries." Henry screamed: "I see the awful immensity of the dangers with which [the constitution] is pregnant. I see it—I feel it. I see *beings* of a higher order anxious concerning our decision." Thunder clapped, the building shook; convention members rushed from their seats outside into the storm (263). Madison's response to Henry's histrionics was to ask for calm reason. At one of the antifederalist's tirades, he replied, "It gives me pain to hear gentlemen continually distorting the natural construction of language, for it is sufficient if any human production can stand a fair discussion."[20]

Madison's calm rationality prevailed, as delegate Bushrod Washington wrote to his uncle at Mount Vernon, saying that Madison spoke with "such force of reasoning, and a display of such irresistible truths, that opposition seemed to have quitted the field."[21] It did not hurt the federalist cause that news of the destruction of weak European confederacies reached the Virginia convention about this time. The Dutch patriot movement had collapsed in the face of French duplicity, Prussian might, and British corruption. "The want of Union and a capable government," Madison wrote, "is the source of all [these] calamities; and particularly of that dependence on foreign powers which is dishonorable to their character as it is destructive of their tranquility."[22] Madison's warnings of the likely disaster if America failed to establish a strong central government with powerful military and diplomatic abilities were borne out again.

Virginia ratified the constitution. Madison's victory was marred by his falling ill to the "bilious lax" that often struck him after particularly intense, stressful periods in his life. He then traveled to New York to witness the forming of the new constitutional government in America and to see what mischiefs human nature might attempt with this new political structure. He did not have to wait long. While the constitution eliminated many of the evils of state autonomy and violations of Lockean individual rights, it was soon used for a new kind of oppression, one growing out of human pride. So Madison's nationalism and Lockean liberalism soon turned to states' rights and classical republicanism in the face of this resourceful human tendency to use political power for wicked purposes.

CHAPTER FIVE

CLASSICAL REPUBLICANISM:

The States' Rights of the
Virginia Resolutions

*The obvious tendency and inevitable result of a consolidation
of the States into one sovereignty, would be to transform the
republican system of the United States into a monarchy.*
— James Madison, 1799

AFTER THE TWO federalist administrations of Presidents George
Washington and John Adams, James Madison perceived a new out-
cropping of evil in American politics, now from an exaggerated national power in the service of arrogant and prideful federal leaders,
displaying itself most prominently in the Alien and Sedition Acts.
Madison's response to this revival of human oppression was the invocation of a classical republican ideology to criticize centralized
and executive political corruption while extolling the virtues of
decentralized authority, states' rights, democratic participation, and
low taxes.

Madison went from a staunch defender of federal power to
combat the splintering dissention of state governments, during and
shortly after the revolution, to the premier advocate, in the 1790s,
of classical republican participatory democracy as the antidote to
an oppressive centralized regime. He remained loyal to a balanced
federal republic in America, one with most domestic policy under
the jurisdiction of the states and localities and foreign policy under the purview of the national government; but he now saw the

greatest threat to justice and stability from inflated federal authority over domestic civil liberties rather than from the disorder and licentiousness of the state autonomy of the 1770s and 1780s.

The origin of political evil, whether state or national, remained the same for Madison, however: human pride and arrogance increased by political power and prestige. The Calvinist catalog of sins—pride, greed, and envy—underlay all the political evils and oppressive measures. Neither decentralized government nor centralized authority were immune from this tendency to be used as instruments for selfish human ends. Under the Articles of Confederation, it had taken the form of local prejudices, legalized theft, popular disorder, and a poor majority fleecing the wealthy minority; under the federalists' conception of the constitution it had evolved into a national aristocracy of proud, privileged financiers and officials stealing from the many and justifying themselves with corrupt legislation and unconstitutional acts. This tendency, begun by Hamilton's national bank and tax proposals, culminated in President John Adams's shielding his foolish vanity with the Alien and Sedition Acts, greatly expanding executive authority and making criticism of his regime a crime. The combination of corrupt political and fiscal policy with insulation from criticism by criminal statute alarmed Madison to the point of his fearing an emergence of monarchy in America. A national regime that could manipulate the economy through corrupt fiscal policy, political patronage, and threats of imprisonment could also pass measures to continue itself in perpetuity. Madison therefore utilized the classical republican strain of American political thought, so effectively used by antifederalists before, against the very federal regime he had helped to establish! This shift in Madison's ideological emphasis, again, was justified by its utility in combating the current, most dangerous tendency against political order and personal liberty—the evil of a national monopoly.

James Madison found in President John Adams the quintessential sinner: proud, vain, arrogant, sensitive to slights, and vicious and authoritarian towards others. His "pompous vanity" soon showed itself in "a scene of ambition beyond all . . . former suspicions and imaginations." Adams's messages to Congress were, to Madison, a series of "violent passions and heretical politics."[1] Comparing the "cool, considerate and cautious" President Washington with Adams, who was "headlong and kindled into flame by every spark that lights on his passion," Madison found the New Englander's "antirepublican discourses" the most "abominable and degrading." He saw the federalists as increasingly "artful and wicked," with Adams's vanity and pride leading the way.[2]

CLASSICAL REPUBLICANISM

Madison's response to these federalist excesses drew upon what the historiographic literature calls the "classical republican paradigm." Developed originally by Historian J. G. A. Pocock, this school of thought emphasizes man's social nature and the need for a small, virtuous, participatory republic of economically independent citizens to secure a healthy, just regime.[3] From the non-British liberal philosophies of Greek and Roman antiquity, especially those of Aristotle and Cicero, this worldview sees a natural cycle of birth, growth, decay, death, and regeneracy in political regimes. A republic is especially susceptible to corruption by centralized authority; standing armies, financial manipulation, and high taxes (transferring wealth from the many virtuous citizens to the few fiscal and political aristocrats); concentration of power in the executive (eventually producing monarchy); and increased reliance upon political appointments or patronage (rather than elected officials accountable to the people). In seventeenth-century England, James Harrington articulates this paradigm, expressing fear over a decadent "court" faction in London robbing the virtuous yeoman "country" citizenry through public credit and debt (the bank), stock markets, high taxes, and increased Parliamentary patronage. Such political degeneracy can only be halted, in this view, by a vigilant defense of founding republican principles: decentralized authority, political participation and civil liberties, economic independence, and frugal government. Several historians see the American Revolution through classical republican lenses, as the preservation of civic virtue against the increasingly corrupt financial imperialism of the British Empire.[4]

This battle continued in the United States as Alexander Hamilton's strategy for national assumption of the state debts, public credit through a national bank, expansion of an army and navy, and concentrated political power in the federal government (especially the executive) met resistance from the antifederalists and Jefferson, who defended the traditional public virtues of states' rights, agrarian economics, legislative supremacy, and a citizen militia. More recent scholarship on classical republicanism, notably that of Michael P. Zuckert and Paul Rahe, asserts a Lockean quality of this republican theory, overcoming the antithesis of liberalism and classicism.[5] Zuckert claims that "the version of republicanism to which the natural rights philosophy pointed was emphatically not classical republicanism" but a version that synthesized ancient and modern qualities (which certainly confirms the synthesis found in Madison). Yet the difference between classical and liberal republicanism remains for Zuckert, and he finds "no simple way to resolve this tension."[6]

James Madison's underlying Augustianism, and its motivating his shifts between Lockean liberalism and classical republicanism, may provide that resolution. Though motivated by, above all, a Christian suspicion of human nature, he saw the federalist policies through these liberal and republican paradigms' ideologies and responded accordingly. In Congress from 1789 to 1797, Madison viewed with alarm the federalist policies of fiscal imperialism and political corruption and consolidation. Madison's shift to states' rights can only be understood in terms of Classical Republicanism.

Madison, in his "Annals of Congress" (February 1791) opposed Hamilton's proposal for a national bank as unconstitutional and an "interference with the powers of the states." "Is the power of establishing an incorporated Bank among the powers vested by the constitution?" he asked. No stretching of the "common defense and general welfare" clause could justify such a violation of strictly enumerated congressional powers, he determined.[7] Madison called the sale of national bank shares a "scramble for so much public plunder" and its salesmen (who he labeled "stock jobbers") base pawns of a corrupt government, "at once its tool and its tyrant; bribed by largesse, and overawing it, by clamours and combinations." He wrote in a newspaper piece (December 3, 1791) of the federalists' "consolidation of the States into one government" and warned of the "incompetency of one Legislature to regulate all the various objects belonging to the local governments." Such "excitements to ambition" looked more and more like "usurpation and oppression" to Madison.[8] Sounding very much like a classical republican, indeed, he identified the federalists as "opulent" and "debauched," relying on "the influence of money and emoluments" as well "the terror of military force."[9] A "paper system" of financial intrigue from New York, combined with concentration of political power in the executive branch in Washington, D.C., led Madison's classical republican ideology to sound a clarion call for resistance from local and state regimes.[10]

The crowning touch of federalist corruption, to Madison, was the "monster" of Adams's Alien and Sedition Acts of 1798. The provisions of these laws capped all the other federalist plans for British-style corruption and monarchy, threatening the foundations of the republic itself. The Alien and Sedition Acts of 1798 represented the height of President Adams's (and the Anglophile federalists') pride and arrogance. His personal sins found expression in this political policy, which granted the executive extraordinary (and unconstitutional) powers and legalized persecution against the regime's opponents, effectively expanding the Presidency into a monarchy and insulating it from criticism or correction. The Alien Bill was aimed at deporting "subversive" (primarily French) elements in America and giving the president extra-constitutional authority to expel all foreigners deemed "dangerous to the peace and safety of the United States."[11] The Sedition Act gave the federal government (especially through the federal courts) power to persecute the administration's internal enemies (Jeffersonian states' rights republicans) by prosecuting the opposition's newspapers. It read, as Madison quoted in his report on the Virginia Resolutions (1799):

> "If any person shall write, print, utter, or publish, or shall cause or procure to be written, printed, uttered, or published, or shall knowingly and willingly assist or aid in writing, printing, uttering, or publishing, any false, scandalous, and malicious writing or writings against the Government of the United States, or the President of the United States, with an intent to defame the said Government or either house of the said Congress, or the Presi-

dent, or to bring them or either of them into contempt or disrepute, or to excite against them, or either or any of them, the hatred of the good people of the United States, etc. — then such person, being convicted before any court of the United States having jurisdiction thereof, shall be punished by a fine not exceeding two thousand dollars, and by imprisonment not exceeding two years."[12]

In other words, the federal government could lock up anyone even remotely connected with criticizing the government. Only a few convictions would serve to produce what the Supreme Court later termed a "chilling effect" on free political speech. The national government, with such a law, could effectively "legally" suppress all opposition to its policies and personnel and rule in perpetuity—that is, the government could establish a monarchy.

Indeed, the federalists used the Sedition Act for just such a purpose. When the Jeffersonian republican newspaper the *Aurora* repeatedly criticized the Adams administration, calling the president the "old, querulous, bald, blind, crippled, toothless Adams," Abigail Adams wrote that it was "cursing and abusing" and wished it to be "suppressed."[13] The federalists then brought court actions against seventeen republican newspapers. No federalist organs were indicted. The *Aurora,* the *Boston Independent Chronicle,* the *New York Argus,* the *Richmond Enquirer,* and four other republican newspapers were prosecuted under the Sedition Act in 1799 alone. Two ceased publication, creating a frightening precedent.

The Jeffersonian response to the Alien and Sedition Acts and the unconstitutional policies they represented was the states' rights documents known as the "Kentucky and Virginia Resolutions." Madison wrote much of the Virginia Resolutions as well as the "Address of the General Assembly" and "Report on the Resolutions," which explicated them. In each, Madison reveals his shift to classical republican ideology against the corrupt regime of the federalists in Washington. They show that he soon saw the greatest expression of human evil and political oppression in the central government and determined that the greatest hope for restoring balance and justice to the American polity was in the state governments.

THE VIRGINIA RESOLUTIONS

In the Virginia Resolution of 1798, Madison states that the decentralized state governments, which form the Union of the national government, could, in extreme cases, "interpose" in blocking unconstitutional acts of the federal regime; "in case of a deliberate, palpable, and dangerous exercise of other powers" not granted by the constitution (or "compact"), "the States, who are parties thereto, have the right and are in duty bound to interpose for arresting the progress of the evil, and for maintaining, within their respective limits, the authorities, rights, and liberties appertaining to them."[14] This did not mean "nullification" of national laws by individual states but rather the combined efforts of the states according to constitutional means of amendment (see chap. 7). Madison expresses "deep regret" that "a spirit" has been manifested "by the Federal Government to enlarge its powers by forced constructions" of the constitution, "so as to consolidate the States, by degrees, into one sovereignty, the obvious tendency and inevitable result of which would be to transform the present republican system of the United States into an absolute, or, at best, a mixed monarchy" (6:327). The resolution goes on to "particularly protest" the "palpable and alarming infractions of the Constitution" in the Alien and Sedition Acts. These acts not only "exercise a power nowhere delegated to the Federal Government" but also actually "subvert the general principles of free government" (6:327–28).

This subversion of the republic, which Madison claims should "produce universal alarm," results from the Sedition Act's crushing the freedoms of speech and press, necessary to open deliberation on public policy and a requisite to an informed electorate voting for candidates. "It is leveled against the right of freely examining public characters and measures, and of free communication among the people . . . which has ever been justly deemed the only effectual guardian of every other right" (6:328–29). The Sedition Act, for Madison, represents the radical altering of the American system of government—from a republic to despotism. Loss of free speech effectively eliminates every other democratic practice. The Virginia ratifying convention "expressly declared that, among other essential rights" in a republic, "the liberty of conscience and of the press cannot be cancelled, abridged, restrained, or modified by any authority of the United States"; therefore Madison implies that the federalist Congress and Adams administration has violated the terms under which Virginia agreed to the constitution. More significant, in terms of Madison's classical republicanism, is his characterization of the national government's "usurpation" as "criminal *degeneracy*" —identifying it with the ancient cycles of birth, growth, decline, and death of regimes. If the "degeneracy" of the republic is not stemmed, corruption and tyranny will ensue in a predictable cycle according to the classical formula (6:329). Thus, a simple statute, like the Sedition Act, could soon become "fatal" to republican government in America. This justifies the state (or Commonwealth) of Virginia declaring it "unconstitutional" (6:331). However, Madison maintained that a state legislature should not "nullify" a federal statute but work in concert with other states to constitutionally alter the offending law.[15]

Address on the Resolutions

In his "Address of the General Assembly to the People of the Commonwealth of Virginia" (1799), Madison explains to the citizens of his state the meaning of the resolutions and the reasons for them. In classical republican style he warns them of the "domestic usurpation" of the Adams administration, which justified under the pretext of foreign danger, soothes "the people into sleep, while that power is swelling, silently, secretly, and fatally." The Sedition Act, he says, "was never expected by the early friends of the Constitution" (of whom he was the leader) when "they admitted that the State sovereignties were only diminished by powers specifically enumerated." Now, "Federal authority is deduced from implication . . . whence Congress will be endowed with a power of legislation in all cases whatsoever, and the States will be stripped of every right reserved, by the concurrent claims of a paramount Legislature." A bitter irony, this is just what Patrick Henry and the antifederalists had predicted during the ratification debates against Madison in Virginia. Likewise, Madison uses almost as dramatic language as Henry when he warns that the Sedition Act will "inflict a death-wound on the Sovereignty of the States" (6:333).

The federalists' employment of the constitution's Preamble to justify these expansions of the national government's power (which Madison, during the ratification debates, had assured opponents could never happen) contradicts the specifically enumerated powers in the body of the document. "Had the States been despoiled of their sovereignty by the generality of the preamble, and had the Federal Government been endowed with whatever they should judge to be instrumental towards union, justice, tranquillity and common defense, general welfare, and the preservation of liberty, nothing could be more frivolous than an enumeration of powers" (6:334).

It is the "frailties of man," their sinful, prideful character, that is at the bottom of these political usurpations and oppression, Madison believed (6:336). Having identified this origin, he enumerates their evils in classical republican terms in the address. The danger lies in "fiscal systems" that "keep a host of commercial and wealthy individuals imbodied, and obedient to the mandates of the treasury" (rather than obedient to God); in "armies and navies" that "enlist the tendency of man to pay homage to his fellow-creatures who can feed or honor him" (rather than paying homage to God Almighty); in "swarms of officers, civil and military, who inculcate political tenets tending to consolidation and monarchy" (i.e., executive patronage); and in the general corruption of the republic to venal and authoritarian activities. "In destroying, by the Sedition Act, the responsibility of public servants and public measures . . . [and] retrograding towards the exploded doctrine 'that the administration of the Government are the masters, and not the servants, of the people,'" the Adams administration is turning towards the cyclical degeneration of the republic, "to the disgrace of returning first to ancient ignorance and barbarism" (6:338–39).

It was talk like this that had motivated Adams to punish seditious language. Madison "shortens the catalogue" of these criminal usurpations by summarizing them as creating "successive precedents" that will eventually "remove every restraint upon Federal power" (6:339–40). Shifting from classical republicanism to his underlying Calvinism, he concludes this address by "humbly and fervently implor[ing] the Almighty Disposer of events to avert from our land war and usurpation, the scourges of mankind"; to allow "virtue" to flourish; to remove "from ambition the means of disturbing the common wealth"; and to "bless our nation with tranquillity, under whose benign influence we may reach the summit of happiness and glory" (6:340).

REPORT ON THE RESOLUTIONS (1799)

James Madison's most elaborate exposition on the Virginia Resolutions and clearest expression of his classical republican ideology remains the sixty-page "Report on the [Virginia] Resolutions," written during the House of Delegates session of 1799–1800. It is a detailed explanation of the Commonwealth's attack on the federalist appropriation of power and a defense against other states' (and federal) government's criticisms of the Virginia Resolutions. In his most penetrating argumentation since the *Federalist Papers*, Madison displays the tight, careful reasoning of his Princeton training, explicating the reasoning behind each component, bolstering each argument with historical, political, and philosophical evidence, elaborating on the objections to its position, and exposing the underlying principles of the federalist subversion of the constitution and the republic. Historian Ralph Ketcham attributes the death of the Alien and Sedition Acts and, by implication, the demise of the federalists in American politics to this tightly reasoned defense of the Virginia Resolutions.[16] Besides refuting the arguments against the resolutions offered by the federalists in Washington, Madison's report addressed criticism from Delaware, Rhode Island, Massachusetts, New York, Connecticut, New Hampshire, and Vermont.

The Virginia Resolutions were widely criticized, first, for asserting that the "states" rather than the "people" formed the constitution (just as Madison had argued in the *Federalist Papers*) and, second, for claiming that the national regime was a "compact" rather than a separate, distinct (and, in its own sphere, independent) government. In his "Report on the Resolutions," Madison makes the almost antifederalist argument that "whatever different construction of the term 'States,' in the resolution, may have been entertained, all will at least concur on the last . . . the Constitution was submitted to the 'States'; in that sense the 'States' ratified it; and in that sense of the term 'States' they are consequently parties to the compact from which the powers of the Federal Government result."[17] Madison (contrary to his earlier federalism) really isn't making the claim that the national regime, as under the Articles of Confederation, is wholly a creature of, and subordinate to, the central government. Rather, he is insisting that the states formed the Union, that, although the government of the Union is now independent (or interdependent), the federal government was formed for distinctive, limited purposes (primarily foreign relations). Now, under the Alien and Sedition Acts, it has expanded beyond those constitutional limits and invaded the jurisdiction (individual civil rights and liberties) of the states, who have principal control over internal politics and domestic policy.

It is in this qualified manner that the resolutions, according to Madison, legitimately allow the states to "interpose for arresting the progress of the evil, and for maintaining within their respective limits the authorities, rights, and liberties appertaining to them" (6:349). Such state interposition should only occur, Madison notes, when federal power affects "vital principles of their political system" (6:350). If the unconstitutional expansion of federal powers into areas of "state sovereignty" did not "justify the parties to it interposing even so far as to arrest the progress of the evil, and thereby to preserve the Constitution," there would be, for Madison, no way to check the usurpation of authority by the national government (6:351). However, as he later argued against John Calhoun's nullification theory, this check was to occur within constitutional means, such as an amendment or a new convention.

Federalists in Washington and in other states rejected this argument, claiming that the national judiciary (Supreme Court) should decide such jurisdictional disputes and the constitutionality of Congressional legislation. Madison answered that (1) there may be instances of usurped authority which the constitution has not placed within the jurisdiction of the federal judiciary; (2) if the sovereignty of the national judicial branch is deemed superior to that of the states that formed the Union, of which it is a part, other national branches may claim similar jurisdiction over the units forming the compact; and (3) the courts themselves may "exercise or sanction dangerous powers beyond the grant of the Constitution" (such as upholding the unconstitutional acts of the Adams administration and prosecuting republican newspapers under the Alien and Sedition Acts), requiring a check from the states as the only barrier to complete national supremacy and tyranny. Without such a decentralized control over central power, there remains no "safeguard against the danger of degeneracy to which republics are liable," writes Madison, in traditional classical republican fashion (6:351, 352).

Another attack on the Virginia Resolutions concerned their failure to recognize that the federalists' expansion of the national government's power was justified by "common defense and general welfare" clauses of the Preamble to the constitution. Madison reserves his greatest contempt for this "forced construction" of the constitutional language and its illegitimate use in the rationalization of the national bank and carriage tax legislation. All of these "misconstructions" of the constitution are, for Madison, "calculated to enlarge the powers of the Federal Government" (6:353, 355). If general phrases are used to negate the limits on the national legislature's jurisdiction, it is evident to Madison "that there is not a single power whatever which may not have some reference to the common defense or general welfare," and so "the government, therefore, which possesses power in either one or other of these extents, is a government without the limitations formed by a particular enumeration of powers; and consequently, the meaning and effect of this particular enumeration is destroyed by the exposition given to these general phrases" (6:356). The result, unless this trend is stopped by state action, would be the total unification of the government in America—the end of federalism and the republic.

This classical republican perception of the impending degenerative doom of liberty brings with it the fear of overall political corruption and decline. "The obvious tendency and inevitable result of a consolidation of the States into one sovereignty . . . [is] to transform the republican system into a monarchy." The "true and fair construction" of these constitutional phrases appears to Madison "too obvious to be mistaken" except by those deliberately distorting the document in order to introduce corruption and monarchy into the system (6:356–57). That is, "the Congress is authorized to provide money for the common defense and general welfare. In both, is subjoined to this authority an enumeration of the cases to which their powers shall extend." Without such a limit to that constitutional construction, all the depravities of monarchy and modern despotism will follow: "excessive augmentation of the offices, honors, and emoluments [i.e., patronage], depending on the Executive [presidential] will. Add to the present legitimate stock all those of every description which a consolidation of the States would take from them and turn over to the Federal government and the patronage of the Executive," and the power and privilege of the central government would be "swelled" beyond all limit (6:357–58).

Madison's "Report on the [Virginia] Resolutions" goes from this general constitutional defense to specific referencing of the most heinous violations by the federalist regime: the Alien and Sedition Acts. The principal problem with the Alien Act, for Madison, is not the deportation of "subversive" French republicans but the unconstitutional granting of power to the executive to deny due process rights. Adding this power (1) "exercises a right nowhere delegated to the Federal Government"; (2) "unites legislative and judicial powers to those of the Executive"; (3) "subverts the general principles of free government"; and (4) "subverts the particular organization and position provisions of the Federal Constitution" (6:360).

Madison punctuates these problems of the Alien Act with an appeal to the constitutional amendment most concerned with states' rights, the Tenth: "That the powers not delegated to the United States by the Constitution, nor prohibited by it to the States, are reserved to the States, respectively, or to the people." While Madison admits the national power in declaring war and in the treatment of "enemy aliens," he reserves internal treatment of nonbelligerent aliens to the states' due process procedures. The judicial due process "held sacred" by the states requires probable cause, witnesses, public trials, and habeas corpus. The Alien Act flouts these state privileges not only by concentrating judicial process at the federal level, violating state procedures, but also by trusting them to "the Executive Magistrate alone," thereby creating a "creeping monarchy." If a suspicion of improper conduct is held by the president alone, "he may order the suspected alien to depart the territory of the United States," in Madison's words (6:361). "They leave everything to the President. His will is law. . . . His suspicion is the only evidence which is to convict; his order, the only judgement which is to be executed" (6:370). Putting it this way, Madison makes the power conferred on the president by the Alien Act sound not just like monarchy but like monarchy based on the divine right of kings, a doctrine sure to alarm American Protestants.

Madison goes on to defend the Virginia Resolutions' rejection of the Sedition Act. Like the Alien Act, (1) "it exercises in like manner a power not delegated by the Constitution"; (2) that presumed power "on the contrary, is expressly and positively forbidden by one of the amendments to the Constitution"; and (3) this power (to legally punish speech and writing critical of the government) "more than any other ought to produce universal alarm, because it is leveled against that right of freely examining public characters and measures, and of free communication . . . which has ever been justly deemed the only effectual guardian of every other right." Madison again advises, as in any examination of national legislation, that "it will be proper to recollect that the Federal Government" is composed of "powers specifically granted" and limited. So, with "a reverence for our Constitution in the true character, in which it issued from the sovereign authority of the people," he finds the new federal laws unwarranted by that document and even subverting elements of it, filling many "with equal astonishment and apprehension" (6:372).

Because the federalist authors of the Sedition Act knew it was not sanctioned by the constitution, they argued that it grew legitimately from the common law tradition: the English system of judicial rulings and precedents that had always sanctioned government censorship and sedition laws in England. Addressing this common law argument provided Madison with an opportunity to elaborate upon the distinctions between English and American law and government. Of course, the attempt to justify federalist legislation by tying the American political system to that of Britain, from which the United States so recently won independence, was enough in itself to cause concern among Americans of all parties. Madison expands on this common law argument, effectively turning it against its advocates. He finds the linking of American politics to the rejected British common law tradition a "novelty" and "extravagant pretension" (6:372). He notes that prior to the revolution, when the states were colonies of the British Empire, the English common law was "made a part of the colonial codes." But, Madison insists, because the different North American colonies were settled at different times under different charters, the English common law "was not the same in any two of the Colonies." Hence, the English common law was never applied uniformly to *all* the colonies together, and so it has no precedent over the whole United States or federal law. So, the colonial "stage of our political history furnishes no foothold for the patrons of this new doctrine," namely that the Sedition Act is legitimated by the common law (6:373).

Madison asks, Did the revolution and establishment of independence introduce the English common law into the law of the United States? The absurdity of this, that separating politically from Britain somehow strengthened the legal traditions between the two countries, Madison shows just by raising the question (6:373). "Such being the ground of our Revolution, no support nor colour can be drawn from it for the doctrine that the common law is binding on these States as one society" (6:374). Then was the English common law introduced by the first compact of the newly independent states, the Articles of Confederation? Having been there and worked under that system, Madison assures us that "no such law is named, or implied or alluded to" in that period of American political history. As United States history develops, Madison finds less and less evidence of an English common law influence on national legislation. "Not a vestige of this extraordinary doctrine can be found in the origin or progress of American institutions," he writes. "The evidence against it has, on the contrary, grown stronger at every step" (6:375).

Was the English common law introduced to American national polity during the formation of the U.S. Constitution? he muses. Again, the absurdity of this is evident to Madison, but he is attempting to remove all supports for the Sedition Act being made legitimate by means of the common law tradition. He therefore looks at the specific constitutional provisions on judicature (Article 3): "The judicial power shall extend to all cases in law and equity arising under this Constitution, the laws of the United States, and treaties made or which shall be made under their authority." Nowhere is English common law mentioned, and "neither of which implies that the common law is the law of the United States," for

Madison (6:376). If "equity" could imply the common law, Madison notes that this system applies only to civil cases "and would exclude cases of criminal jurisdiction"—that is, the prosecutions under the Sedition Act (6:377).

To finish off this fairly dead horse, Madison examines some of the "difficulties and confusion" with admitting the English common law as the basis of American federal law. Is it with or without the British statutory law emerging from the common law? When should the British common law end in influencing American politics? At the date of the oldest colony? The youngest colony? Perhaps at the date of our independence? "Or are the dates to be thrown together and a medium deduced?" (6:379). Should the English common law be applied to all state laws or just federal law? A careful examination of the implications and consequences of America adopting the British common law quickly shows Madison that the federalist argument that common law justifies the Sedition Act is ridiculous. "The difficulties and uncertainties incident to the doctrine; and of its vast consequences in extending the powers of the Federal Government, and in superseding the authorities of the State Government" proves "the common law never was, nor by any fair construction ever can be, deemed a law for the American people." Madison "indulges" the strongest expectation that others will soon come to the same conclusion, and he frankly finds it "distressing to reflect" that anyone would ever entertain such an absurd idea (6: 381, 382).

Next Madison addresses the federalist claim that the enlarged national authority provided by the Alien and Sedition Acts, and other legislation, is allowed by the expansive language of the Preamble to the U.S. Constitution. He reasons that any "Preamble usually contains the general motives or reasons for the particular regulations or measures which follow it, and is always understood to be explained and limited by them" (6:382). In its "fair and consistent meaning" the Preamble to the constitution, or any other general phrase, "cannot enlarge the enumerated powers vested in Congress." The "necessary and proper" clause does not itself contain a grant of powers to the Congress, it is only "the means of carrying into execution those otherwise granted" by the specific enumerated powers given Congress in Article 2 of the constitution (6:382). Finally, in the "Report on the [Virginia] Resolutions," Madison asks if the Sedition Act is forbidden by one of the amendments to the constitution. The First Amendment says that "Congress shall make no law . . . abridging the freedom of speech or of the press." Critics of the Virginia Resolutions attempted to vindicate the Sedition Act by claiming that "abridging" meant censoring or applying "prior restraint" but did not prevent subsequent persecution (6:385–86). Madison replies that this misinterpretation of "freedom of the press" derives from the British common law and monarchical political philosophy contrary to the distinctive American idea of freedom of expression. This gives Madison another opportunity to explicate, in a classical republican manner, the differences between American and British views of liberty, government, and the executive.

The British Constitution (which is unwritten) views encroachments of rights exclusively from the point of view of the "executive magistrate." Parliament is seen as unlimited in its power, or omnipotent. Hence, the English "ramparts for protecting the rights of the people" (the Magna Carta, the Bill of Rights, etc.) are raised against royal prerogative only. In the United States, however, Madison notes that "the People, not the Government, possess absolute sovereignty" (6:386). The legislature, as well as the executive, are under limitations of power, prevented from encroaching upon the individual, God-given rights of nature, including freedom of thought and communication. These are secured "against legislative as well as executive ambition," in Madison's words. The security of the freedom of the press "requires that it should be exempt not only from previous restraint by the Executive, as in Great Britain, but from legislative restraint also; and this exemption, to be effectual, must be an exemption not only from the previous inspection of licensers, but from subsequent penalty of laws" (6:387). The underlying (classical republican and Christian) assumption for Madison is that America supposes "a greater freedom of animadversion than might be tolerated by the genius of such a government as that of Great Britain." This is simply because the hereditary monarchy is considered infallible, it "can do no wrong," whereas the American president is considered fallible, as imperfect as the rest of humanity and therefore should be limited as any other man. "In the United States," Madison notes, "the executive magistrates are not held to be infallible nor the

Legislature to be omnipotent; and both being elective, are both responsible" for not invading the individual rights of the citizens (6:388). Deriving from his Christian perspective that all men are fallen, none Godlike, it follows that no human individual should have absolute authority. Consequently, the presumption is for individual rights of expression rather than for the dignity of rulers.

Despite abuses of freedom of the press, Madison argues, as Jefferson did, that, overall, its positive effects outweigh the negative. "Some degree of abuse is inseparable from the proper use of a thing, and in no instance is this more true than in that of the press," but "it is better to leave a few of its noxious branches to their luxuriant growth, than, by pruning them away, to injure the vigour of those yielding the proper fruits." To the press alone, Madison insists, "the world is indebted for all the triumphs which have been gained by reason and humanity over error and oppression." Had legislation like the Sedition Act forbid every publication which "might bring" governmental authorities "into contempt or disrepute," Madison muses, the United States might not have been delivered from "the infirmities of a sickly Confederation" or even evolved beyond "miserable colonies groaning under a foreign yokes" (6:389).

Reviewing the reasoning of federalist arguments in support of the Sedition Act, Madison makes a remark reminiscent of his consternation over Patrick Henry's histrionics at the ratifying convention: "It is painful to remark how much the arguments now employed in behalf of the Sedition Act are at variance with the reasoning which then justified the Constitution, and invited its ratification" (6:390). At that ratifying convention, Madison notes, Virginia specifically urged the adoption of amendments guaranteeing individual rights as an implicit condition for ratification. He quotes the Virginia Ratifying Convention's instructions as later expressed by the first Congress, that "the Conventions of a number of the States having, at the time of their adopting the Constitution, expressed a desire, in order to prevent misconstructions or abuse of its powers, that further declaratory and restrictive clauses should be added" (6:391). Madison is implying that the federalists' Sedition Act betrays the trust of the states that ratified the constitution and breaches the social contract. In other words, the federalists have violated the constitution. "The construction employed to justify the

Sedition Act would exhibit a phenomenon without a parallel in the political world," according to Madison, if it is not checked and corrected. This state correction of the abuse of federal power will, for Madison, "account for the policy of binding the hand of the Federal Government from touching the channel which alone can give efficacy to its responsibility to its constituents" (6:392, 393).

The worst excess of the Sedition Act, for Madison, is its corrosive effect on the republic—a system of government premised on the popular selection of leaders. That selection "can only be determined by a free examination . . . and a free communication among the people" (6:394). He notes that since the Sedition Act was passed, in July 1798, there had been two elections of the House of Representatives, one for part of the Senate, and one for president. The purpose of these elections was to "preserve the purity or to purge the faults of the Administration," which are "the great remedial rights of the people." But under the shadow of the Sedition Act, the free—and often critical—discussion of the national leaders was inhibited by fear of criminal persecution. Hence, Madison concludes, "may it not be asked of every intelligent friend to the liberties of his country, whether the power exercised in such an act . . . ought not to produce great and universal alarm?" (6:394–95). A "rigid execution" of the Sedition Act could "repress that information and communication among the people which is indispensable to the just exercise of their electoral rights," effectively ending republicanism and causing the government to degenerate into tyranny, as any established administration would be able to perpetuate their rule indefinitely. Applied consistently, such a law will effectively "destroy our free system of government" (6:395). A government "thus entrenched" can easily "evade the responsibility which is essential to a faithful discharge of its duty." Honest republican government, given the frailty and sinfulness of men, needs the check of the free press. "The right of electing the members of the Government constitutes more particularly the essence of a free and responsible government," and this right "depends on the knowledge of the comparative merits and demerits of the candidates for public trust, and on the equal freedom, consequently, of examining and discussing these merits and demerits of the candidates" (6:397).

Madison concludes his "Report on the [Virginia] Resolutions" by returning to the theme of his earliest political writings: freedom of religion. If the central government can pass laws restricting the essential freedoms of speech and press despite their constitutional protections, it can pass a law establishing a national church despite the freedom of religion clause in the constitution. "A palpable violation of one of those rights—the freedom of the press . . . may be fatal to the other—the free exercise of religion" (6:400). The specter of a revived Anglican establishment looms large in Madison's conclusion, producing a fear in Virginia's newly freed evangelical Christians (Baptists and Methodists), fear that in 1800 translated into votes for the Jeffersonian republicans. Madison finds the federalists' employment of English common law in justifying the Sedition Act particularly ominous in light of those desiring to reestablish the official Church of England (6:401).

Madison ends his most classical republican writings on states' rights with a justification for states exercising such a check on national power, to ensure a balanced, healthy republic of citizens "who apprehend danger to liberty from the establishment of the General Government over so great a country [and] to the vigilance with which they would decry the first symptoms of usurpation" (6:405). His last words in the report encourage other states to "renew their protest against 'the Alien and Sedition Acts,' as palpable and alarming infractions of the Constitution" (6:406).

CHAPTER SIX

NATIONALISM REVISITED

*No People ought to feel greater obligations to celebrate the
goodness of the Great Disposer of Events and of the Destiny
of Nations than the people of the United States.*
—James Madison, 1815

JAMES MADISON returned to national public service in 1801, first
as President Jefferson's Secretary of State and then as a two-term
president himself. With the central government's exercising control
over international relations and a universal domestic economy,
Madison found himself, as he had during the Continental Congress,
focusing on national political power. The Louisiana Purchase, the
Embargo act, and the United States Bank brought out Madison's
appreciation of the need for vigorous central authority and the
evils of national political weakness, especially when facing war, foreign threats, or economic chaos. Throughout this period, however,
Madison's Calvinist realism prompted him to balance decentralized,
state control over internal policy (based on classical republican
principles), with centralized, national authority over external affairs
(based on Lockean liberal terms of the right to governmental "self-
preservation"). Yet, after a long period of increased nationalism, he
returned to strict federalist constructionism at the very end of his
presidency and public career.

With the election of Thomas Jefferson as president in 1801, James
Madison found himself back in national politics, this time as Secre-

tary of State. This made him the closest official to the president, the "second in command," as the office of Secretary of State was more prominent than that of vice president in the early nineteenth century, when candidates did not run on a joint ticket. Because most American politics was domestic, and therefore under the jurisdiction of the state governments, the Department of State that Madison oversaw was limited to international matters appropriated to the central federal government. Its staff consisted of one chief clerk, seven subordinate clerks, and a messenger—all located in the same executive office. In addition to its foreign responsibilities, the State Department oversaw some internal policies of a national nature: patents, the census, custody of public documents, printing of Congressional statutes, and keeping the great seal of the United States.[1]

Still, despite the limited size, scope, and resources of the U.S. State Department, Madison found himself swamped with paperwork. He personally corresponded with American ambassadors and consuls around the world, dealt with foreign ministers in Washington, issued passports and ships' papers, and rescued wayward American travelers and seamen. Secretary Madison felt almost overwhelmed by administrative duties. "I find myself in the midst of arrears of papers, etc. etc., which little accord with my unsettled health," he soon wrote. His private correspondence was halted by "the mass of business in the department, at all times considerable, swelled to an unusual size by Sundry temporary causes."[2]

During his term as Secretary of State, Madison dealt with two significant political issues relative to American federalism and his own political philosophy: the Louisiana Purchase, by which the national government acquired land equal in size to the existing United States (an acquisition unprovided for in the enumerated constitutional powers of the Union), and the Embargo Act, which gave the central federal government extraordinary powers to regulate economic activity throughout the country by prohibiting commerce with other nations. Interpreting both as international issues, Madison justified these powerful political acts as under the federal government's jurisdiction, despite objections from both federalists and some republicans that they represented excessive overreaching of national powers.

THE LOUISIANA PURCHASE

Madison shared Thomas Jefferson's hope for ultimately expanding republican government throughout the Western Hemisphere, establishing an "empire of liberty" in North and South America, one freed from European monarchy, decadence, and religious tyranny. So, when the exceedingly complex international negotiations between rival French, Spanish, and British empires provided the United States with an opportunity to acquire the immense territory east and west of the Mississippi River, both Jefferson and Madison approved the Louisiana Purchase. This effectively doubled the size of the country at a cost of about thirteen cents an acre. It was an extraordinary coup for the young nation in expanding its borders, wealth, and future power and influence; but it tested both Jefferson's and Madison's strict constructionist constitutionalism and stretched their federalist ideology.

Since the power of acquiring new land was not specifically given to the federal government by the U.S. Constitution, Jefferson's strict constructionism led him to prefer a constitutional amendment to allow the national government to acquire the land. Madison, who had coordinated the purchase negotiations with Spain and France, regarded the acquisition as purely an international treaty, fully within the purview of the federal government. He concurred with Secretary of Treasury Albert Gallatin's argument that "the existence of the United States as a nation presupposes the power enjoyed by every nation of extending their territory by treaties."[3] Madison wrote to U.S. negotiator Robert Livingston in Paris that the purchase of western lands claimed by France was "in every view . . . a most precious acquisition."[4] To Charles Pickney, American minister to Spain, he wrote: "I repeat to you the wish of the president that every effort and address be employed to obtain the arrangement by which the territory on the East Side of the Mississippi including New Orleans may be ceded to the United States."[5] The final extent of the land acquisition greatly exceeded what Madison originally had understood by the agreement, eventually including the vast area between the Mississippi River and the Rocky Mountains. Of this, he wrote to the negotiators, "It was not presumed that more could be sought by the United States, either with a chance of success, or perhaps without being suspected of greedy ambition."⁶ Such an enormous expansion of the country's territory, with the protection it afforded the United States from hostile foreign neighbors, greatly increased, for Madison, the justification of national authority, despite unclear constitutional delegation of powers.

President Jefferson still preferred a constitutional amendment to secure the sale, telling Gallatin, "I think it will be safer not to permit the enlargement of the Union but by amendment of the Constitution."⁷ Jefferson was already being dubbed "the Grand Turk" by his federalist opponents for this use of national power, and he was sensitive to the charge of hypocrisy. "When an instrument admits two constructions," he wrote, "the one safe, the other dangerous, the one precise, the other indefinite, I prefer that which is safe and precise. I had rather ask an enlargement of power from the nation where it is found necessary, than to assume it by a construction which would make our powers boundless" (97). When delays in Congressional ratification of the purchase raised threats that France and or Spain would renege on the deal, however, Jefferson acquiesced to "expediency" and acted in his executive prerogative over foreign relations (96). When Senator John Quincy Adams criticized the administration for acting without constitutional authority, Madison simply reminded him of "the magnitude of the object."⁸ Federalists going beyond the constitution to pass a Sedition Act designed to persecute their political opponents and contrary to state protections of civil rights was a clear violation of the U.S. Constitution; Republicans exercising legitimate national (and executive) authority in foreign relations to acquire a valuable expansion of the nation's territory required no such specific constitutional provision. The purchase was consistent with Madison's view of American federalism—that the states dealt with internal policies and the central government with external policy. To Madison, negotiations with foreign powers to acquire contiguous land constituted international relations.

THE EMBARGO

The Embargo Act of 1807 came in response to European restrictions on international trade, which had been enacted as part of the war effort between Britain and France. Prior to that time, American shipping had enjoyed a semblance of neutrality amongst hostile European powers and, with it, increasing prosperity. But in 1807, Napoleon's Berlin Decree punished all trade not allied to France, and George III ordered British vessels to continue plundering neutral shipping and impressing sailors.[9] Both commands represented maritime war. The United States, which had almost no navy, was not prepared for naval warfare on a European scale in order to protect its shipping. The Jefferson administration instead employed commercial retaliation: through the Nonimportation Act of December 14, 1807, which prohibited importation of goods to America from belligerents; and through the Embargo Act of December 22, 1807, which prohibited American shipping to foreign countries. The embargo affected about 1,500 American ships, 20,000 American seamen, and almost $60,000,000 worth of cargo.[10] Obviously, most of the economic distress it caused was centered on northeastern shipping interests and coastal cities (a fact not lost on the predominantly federalist New Englanders, who saw it as a direct attack by Jefferson on republican opponents). To Madison, however, it was a civilized, new, republican foreign policy alternative to war.

As early as his college days at Princeton, Madison had advocated nonimportation agreements as an affective remedy to ensure colonial rights. As a member of Congress from 1789 to 1794, Madison repeatedly had proposed American commercial restrictions on British goods as retaliation for English misbehavior. He believed this could be a powerful tool, since the livelihoods of hundreds of thousands of British workmen and merchants depended on goods sold to the United States and the British West Indies depended on American lumber and foodstuffs. Additionally, the loss of European imports would stimulate American domestic manufacture and reduce reliance upon European luxuries (also reducing, by implication, monarchical and "Catholic" decadence).[11] Jefferson too seemed especially keen on the social benefits of isolating America's "sturdy republican virtue" from European corruption and pollution.[12] Throughout his term as Secretary of State, Madison maintained his prejudice against monarchical, feudal, Catholic Spain (the power that had been responsible for the Inquisition). When the Spanish intendant at New Orleans tried to close the port to American shipping, Madison characterized him "as obstinate as he has been ignorant or wicked"; when the Spanish ambassador stormed into Madison's Washington office and accused the secretary of an "atrocious libel" on his country, Madison calmly told him that such "intemperance and disrespect" would not be tolerated.[13]

Unfortunately, the coastal cities and shipping businesses dependent on international commerce (especially in the Northeast) suffered economic privations and saw the republican Embargo Act as targeting federalist regions and abusing federal power. While Madison viewed the embargo as a legitimate federal control over foreign affairs, his opponents felt it was domestic economic despotism with political overtones. As American opposition to the embargo increased, Jefferson responded severely, earning himself the epitaph "Thomas the First." He pressured the Governor of Massachusetts (the state in which most smuggling was occurring) to reduce food imports and dispatched federal gunboats off the eastern seaboard to capture smugglers. Infuriated by illegal trade across the Canadian border, he ordered the Governor of Vermont to "crush these audacious proceedings, and make the offenders feel the consequences of individuals daring to oppose the law by force . . . no effort should be spared to compass the object.[14] No longer did he chuckle about "a little rebellion, now and then" being good for "the tree of liberty." Rather, Jefferson's harsh reactions to resistance to the embargo seemed to confirm to federalists (and increasingly, to his fellow republicans in Congress) that the policy was politically motivated, hypocritical, and vindictive.

Madison's rationale for the embargo policy was of purer motives, and he really thought it had the "solid support in the judgment and patriotic pride of the great body of the nation."[15] There was no alternative save that of war or national humiliation at the hands of British and French navies. "Would war be a better resort?" he asked. "That would be a calamity to the United States."[16] Still, by late summer of 1808, Madison began to see the handwriting on the wall as support for the embargo dwindled. He saw more and more "malignant partizans" who "flinched from . . . duty."[17] He could not believe the "depravity and stupidity" of shortsighted New Englanders who wanted to repeal the Embargo Act. Madison, with his Calvinist tenets, could only attribute it to "their ambitious or vindictive view." Unfortunately, this "factious spirit" continued, raising petitions to Congress for repeal, widespread subversion of the law, and threats of succession. To New Englanders suffering severely from the embargo, this "peaceful coercion" was not working; the British and French empires were not so dependent on American trade as the Jeffersonians presumed, and all the policy was doing was ruining the American economy. Madison finally admitted that "the Eastern seaboard is become so impatient under privations of activity and gain . . . that it becomes necessary for the sake of the Union that the spirit not be too much opposed." When the Embargo Act was repealed, he insisted it was "the disorganizing spirit in the East" that was to blame and concluded that "war is inevitable."[18]

MADISON AS PRESIDENT

The war came in 1812. British harassment of neutral American shipping just became "too absurd and insulting" for Madison.[19] French blockades and piracy also violated American trade, but Madison, in classic Calvinist language, claimed that "the original sin against neutrals lies with Great Britain."[20] In his address promoting a Congressional declaration of war against Britain, Madison enumerates the "series of acts, hostile to the United States, as an Independent and neutral nation." British cruisers "have been in the continued practice of violating the American flag . . . and of seizing and carrying off persons sailing under it." Against this "crying enormity" the United States had unsuccessfully remonstrated (298). "To the most insulting pretentions," Madison adds, "they have added the most lawless proceedings in our very harbors; and have wantonly spilt American blood, within the sanctuary of our territorial jurisdiction." He laments that "our commerce has been plundered . . . our country [has] been cut off from their legitimate markets; and a destructive blow aimed at our agricultural and maritime interests." He continues, pointing out that "not content with these occasional expedients for laying waste our neutral trade, the cabinet of Great Britain resorted, at length, to the sweeping system of Blockades, under the orders in Council; which has been mounded and managed, as might best suit its political views, its commercial jealousies, or the avidity of British cruisers" (299). He concludes that this naval piracy, along with the inciting of Indian "Savages" (whose warfare he notes is "distinguished by features peculiarly shocking to humanity") has put Great Britain in "a state of war against the United States" (300–301).

In June 1812, Congress declared war on Great Britain. Madison saw this as a part of international policy, wholly within the jurisdiction of the federal central government and that of the executive branch as well. He ordered troops into Spanish Florida by executive writ, effectively annexing the territory for the United States.[21] He resented New England's resistance to the war, especially state governors' refusing to allow federal control of state militia in areas outside their native regions. Madison was disappointed by this obstruction of the "National will."[22] After a long, inconclusive, and often humiliating war, the Treaty of Ghent (1815) ended hostilities with Britain on terms only slightly more favorable than conditions before the commencement of war. Still, as President Madison provided a Thanksgiving Proclamation expressing the need for "devout acknowledgements of Almighty God for His great goodness manifested in restoring to them the blessings of peace,"[23] he used the occasion to rehearse his Providential view of American history:

No People ought to feel greater obligations to celebrate the goodness of the Great Disposer of Events and of the Destiny of Nations than the people of the United States. His kind providence originally conducted them to one of the best portions . . . for the great family of the human race. He protected and cherished them under all their difficulties and trials. . . . Under His fostering care their habits, their sentiments, and their pursuits prepared them for a transition in due time to a state of independence and self government . . . distinguished by multiplied tokens of His benign interposition. . . . He reared them into the strength and endowed them with the resources which have enabled them to assert their national rights and to enhance their national character in another arduous conflict . . . now so happily terminated by a peace and reconciliation with those who have been our enemies. And to the same Divine Author of Every Good and Perfect Gift [James 1:17] we are indebted for all those privileges and advantages, religious as well as civil; which are so richly enjoyed in this land.[24]

War had caused many sufferings during Madison's presidency, but he expressed gratitude in his State of the Union address in 1813 for "the numerous blessings with which our beloved Country continues to be favored . . . above all for the light of divine truth."[25] His New Light theology permeated this crisis period.

THE BANK

Despite his classical republican critique of a national bank in the 1790s as a tool of fiscal corruption and centralized oppression, Madison began to modify his opinion of the utility and constitutionality of the Bank of the United States during his presidency. Knowing the controversial nature of this issue, Madison maintained a "neutral" attitude on the subject and let his Treasury Secretary, Albert Gallatin, lead the fight for reestablishment of the bank.[26] Though it later brought accusations of duplicity, this strategy initially produced praise for Madison's principles, as evidenced in a letter from Samuel Carswell in 1811:

> I beg leave to congratulate you, on the decision of the U.S. Bank question, as it is so favorable to the future welfare of this Country, & is another triumph of American Virtue, over British corruption & intrigue. It must be obvious to every one, who has the least knowledge of that Bank & is not willfully blind, that it has always been under the influence of those who are inimical to the Republican principles of this Government—that it is partial in the distribution of its favors. . . . No institution, capable of extending its influence so greatly, as the U.S. Bank was one-third of establishing that influence, by so powerful a motive, as a sense of dependence in those connected with it, should be suffered to exist in this Country. If we must have monied in-

stitutions, Congress cannot use too much care to render them harmless; that the people may enjoy the benefits arising from them, without having their independence shackled & this can be effected in no other way, than by preventing any one, from having a superiority to the rest, in point of privilege & power.[27]

This archetypical classical republican critique of a national bank as a bastion of privilege and corruption had made sense to Madison before he was president. Now he saw the convenience and relatively benign character of the bank, so long as a republican Congress regulated it. Treasury Secretary Gallatin revealed this convenience to President Madison when in 1810 he faced the dissolution of the First Bank of the United States and the necessity (and expense) of transferring its assets to other banking institutions. He wrote to Madison: "I enclose for your signature an authority in the usual form empowering me to negotiate a loan with the Bank of the United States, if you approve of the terms which I had proposed. . . . If the Charter is not renewed, a loan to the same amount (3,750,000 dollars) must be negotiated in 1811, to repay this. If the Charter is renewed, nothing more will be necessary than annually to renew the loan" (2:361).

Secretary Gallatin sent a similar letter to Madison dated February 26, 1811, exposing the difficulties associated with the loss of the central bank (3:184–85). Madison acknowledged these inconveniences to Gallatin in his letter of August 14, 1810, in which he said "I understand that the measures taken by the Bank of the U.S. for provisionally winding up its affairs, are likely to bear hard on the other Banks, and that the evil will be increased, by the drain on the Charter for paying the bonds, as they become due in the hands of the former." He observes in the same letter that this "embarrassment" will fall on "farmers and planters" as much as on "the Monied interest," showing that the integrated national economy managed by the U.S. Bank was now benefitting common people as well as the financial aristocracy, so long as it was held accountable to a Jeffersonian republican Congress (2:483–84).

As Madison softened his attitude on the national bank, he was soon criticized by the localized constituency. As article in the *Baltimore* stated that if JM has changed his views because he now follows "federal precedents" and "the petty-fogging rules of courts," then the Republicans struggled for their principles in vain and politics is "nought but a contest for loaves and fishes,—an ignoble squabble between *ins* and *outs* . . . that liberty has been lost by "avarice, by intrigue, by timidity, by all the corruption which peace and commerce are too apt to engender! Must we too, after passing through the red sea of revolution, perish in the desert?" (2:305)

When Madison finally came out openly for the rechartering of the Bank of the United States in late 1815, he justified it constitutionally through the Congressional authority to establish a uniform currency (Article 1, Section 8): "It is . . . essential, to every modification of the finances, that the benefits of an uniform national currency should be restored to the community. . . . If the operation of the State Banks cannot produce this result, the probable operation of a National bank will merit consideration."[28] This circumspection in December of 1815 was clarified finally when Madison signed a bill rechartering the (second) Bank of the United States in April 1816. In the same year, he advocated the very non–classical republican causes of an increased army, a national University, and a military academy, along with certain internal improvements.[29] All of these policies, none of which were enumerated in the constitution, were justified for Madison by the War of 1812 and by the needs of a growing national economy. He felt these policies would be safe as long as they were regulated by a virtuous Jeffersonian republican Congress. As always, in Madison's realistic view, avoiding a greater evil (military unpreparedness, economic dependence on hostile countries, etc.) was more important than rigid, unthinking adherence to abstract principle.

Many years later, in a letter of 1831, Madison tried to rationalize his changed approach to the bank, saying, "the constitutionality of the power I still regard as sustained by the considerations to which I yielded in giving my assent to the existing Bank." He argued that this constitutional validity "turns on the question how far legislative precedents, expounding the Constitution, ought to guide succeeding Legislatures."[30] If a needed institution (like the national bank) is not specifically provided for in the constitution, but "the uniform sanction of successive legislative bodies through a period of years and under the varied ascendancy of parties" accept it, establishing that institution may not be unconstitutional (392). Obviously Madison emphasized "the practical judgement" of a law over an area that the constitution is silent, and he trusted in the wisdom of Congressional representatives to base sound policy on legitimate statutory precedent. This extra-constitutional legislative action does not apply if laws are explicitly contrary to the founding document, as a "Constitution being derived from a superior authority, is to be expounded and obeyed, not controlled or varied, by the subordinate authority of a Legislature." Likewise, a single Congressional session "differing in the construction of the Constitution from a series of preceding constructions" does not have the validity of several legislative precedents, and so "they not only introduce uncertainty and instability in the Constitution, but in the laws themselves" (391). The consistent Congressional support for the Bank of the United States provided, for Madison, a legitimate justification for its constitutionality, as he summarized:

> It was in conformity with the view here taken, of the respect due to deliberate and reiterated precedents, that the Bank of the United States, though on the original question held to be unconstitutional, received the Executive signature in the year 1817. The act originally establishing a bank had undergone ample discussions in its passage through the several branches of the Government. It had been carried into execution throughout a period of twenty years with annual legislative recognition . . . indeed, . . . with the entire acquiescence of all the local authorities, as well as of the nation at large; to all of which may be added, a decreasing prospect of any change in the public opinion adverse to the constitutionality of such an institution. (393)

So, the combination of repeated legislative support of a policy (under different party influence), the practical necessity of an institution to an effective administration of the federal government, continued popular support of the measure (including state and local branches), and the absence of direct constitutional opposition to the policy allows, for Madison, the adding of federal programs not specifically enumerated in the U.S. Constitution. He believed that the United States Bank met all of these requirements. With such compelling support, a rigid adherence to limited constitutional provisions would be a sin of stubborn pride. So, he became more flexible in constitutional interpretation than some of his strict constructionist colleagues (like Thomas Jefferson or John Taylor).

However, in 1817, as he saw the Congressional republicans getting carried away with national power, Madison reasserted his strict constructionism of the constitution. In his last act as president, he vetoed a bill for extensive federal internal improvements, citing a caution reminiscent of his 1790s classical republicanism:

> The legislative powers vested in Congress are specified and enumerated in the eighth section of the first article of the Constitution, and it does not appear that the power proposed to be exercised by the bill is among the enumerated powers, or that it falls by any just interpretation within the power to make laws necessary and proper for carrying into execution those or other powers vested by the Constitution in the Government of the United States. . . . To refer the power in question to the clause "to promote for the common defense and general welfare" would be contrary to the established and consistent rules of interpretation, as rendering the special and careful enumeration of powers which follow the clause nugatory and improper. Such a view of the Constitution would have the effect of giving to Congress a general power of legislation instead of the defined and limited one hither to understood to belong to them, the terms "common defense and general welfare" embracing every object and act within the purview of a legislative trust. It would have the effect of subjecting both the Constitution and the laws of the several States in all cases, not specifically exempted to superceded by the laws of Congress.[31]

James Madison left the White House and his active political career with a return to his second stage of political ideology—classical republican theory (in favor of states' rights); or rather, he returned to the balanced federalism in which centralized and decentralized governments balanced each other, limiting the excessive evils, prompted by human sin, of both. This sense of balance between competing excesses emerged most eloquently in his political writing after his retirement from public life.

CHAPTER SEVEN

LAST TESTAMENTS

In order to understand the true character of the Constitution of the United States, the error, not uncommon, must be avoided, of viewing it through the medium, either of a Consolidated Government, or of a Confederated Government, whilst it is neither the one nor the other; but a mixture of both.

—James Madison, 1830

IN RETIREMENT, James Madison enjoyed a remarkably pleasant, productive, and yet political last twenty years of life. Punctuated by rural activities, visits from guests from around the world, a voluminous correspondence, and political advising and activity, Madison's "retirement" was almost as busy as the first seventy years of his life. His unusually happy family life was disturbed only by his stepson, Payne Todd, whose frequent drunkenness, extravagant gambling debts, and dissipation constituted what a family friend called a veritable "serpent in the Garden of Eden" during Madison's last years.[1] Still, most of Madison's domestic life was felicitous, surrounded by a loving wife and other devoted family members. Friends in the vicinity of his estate, Montpellier, included Thomas Jefferson, with whom he regularly corresponded and frequently visited.

Madison was often consulted on political matters, especially international ones, by his successor to the presidency, James Monroe.[2] Sensitive to the charge of meddling in politics in his retired condition and the suspicion at times that he was growing senile, Madison wrote to N. P. Trist in 1830 that "a man whose years have but reached the canonical three-score-and-ten (and mine are much beyond the number) should distrust himself, whether distrusted by his friends or not, and should never forget that his arguments . . . will be answered by allusions to the date of his birth."[3] Still, he advised the federal government on American diplomacy, the tariff, Floridian borders, and internal improvements.[4] He served as a delegate to the state convention revising the Virginia constitution, succeeded Thomas Jefferson as Rector of the University of Virginia, and joined a society (made up primarily of clergymen) devoted to aiding Native Americans in the areas of agriculture, education, and religion (633–34).

These public activities and frequent writings on current affairs did not inhibit Madison's more leisurely lifestyle on his Virginia plantation. His farming interests dominated his letters, with talk of fields, crops, weather, and the marketing of produce (621). He delighted in the beautiful mountains and valleys of Piedmont Virginia surrounding his estate. In an address to the local agricultural society, he emphasized the healthy qualities of rural life as opposed to the unhealthy environment of crowded cities and stale air. "In all confined situations," he wrote, "from the dungeon to the crowded work-house, and from these to the compact population of overgrown cities, the atmosphere becomes, in corresponding degrees, unfitted by reiterated use, for sustaining human life and health." As Jefferson had said earlier, in reflecting on the crowded cities of Europe, especially Paris, America's blessed abundance of land and space lent itself to free, republican government. However, Madison clarified, "the enviable condition of the United States is often too much ascribed to the physical advantages of their soil and climate, and to their uncrowded situation. Much is certainly due to these causes, but a just estimate of the happiness of our country will never overlook what belongs to the fertile activity of a free people, and the benign influence of a responsible Government" (622).

Several visitors to Madison's estate during his retirement recorded his appearance and routine, revealing both his private habits and his public personality. A young Harvard professor, George Ticknor, visited Madison with Daniel Webster in 1824 and described his home as on "a very fine, commanding situation, with the magnificent range of the Blue Ridge stretching along the whole horizon." Of Madison himself, Ticknor wrote, "He lives, apparently, with great regularity. We breakfasted at nine, dined about four, drank tea at seven and went to bed at ten. . . . From ten o'clock in the morning till three we rode, walked, or remained in our rooms."[5] Another guest wrote of Madison that "he looks scarcely as old as he is . . . and seems very hale and hearty—the expression of his face is full of good humour—he was dressed in black, with breeches and old fashioned top boots, which he afterwards took off and sat during the evening in his white stockings . . . his favorite topic appeared . . . to be the early constitutional history of his country . . . the constitution . . . etc."[6] An Italian visitor described Madison in 1825 as old and thin but "of a kindly and pleasant face; his bearing is very aristocratic, and without assuming the air of importance and dignity befitting one of his station, he displays an indescribable gentleness and charm." This Count Vidua went on to pronounce Madison's mind extremely keen: "I have heard few people speak with such precision." When he compared the two Virginia presidents, Vidua said that "Jefferson's intellect seemed . . . the most brilliant, Madison's the most profound"; he preferred the latter because Madison's "reflections seemed . . . the most weighty, denoting a great mind and a good heart" (621).

Washington D.C. socialite Margaret Bayard Smith found Madison "living History" in 1828. At the dinner table he spoke of the leading figures and events in America's founding, and when she retired to bed she "felt as if [her] mind was full to overflowing . . . as if [she] had feasted to satiety" (620). Mrs. Smith also noted Madison's notorious droll sense of humor and remarked that the company often laughed heartily. Several others noted the elder Madison's combination of gravity on important (political) subjects and levity over many domestic matters. Bookseller Samuel Whitcomb found Madison "very sociable, rather jocose, quite sprightly, and active . . . less studied, brilliant and frank but more natural, candid and profound than Mr. Jefferson. . . . Mr. Madison has a sound judgement, tranquil temper and logical mind . . . nothing in his looks, gestures, expressions or manners to indicate anything extraordinary in his intellect or character, but the more one converses with him, the more his excellences are developed and the better he is liked" (630). Charles Ingersoll said that "a purer, brighter, juster spirit has seldom existed" (669). An illustration of Madison's penchant for telling amusing stories and laughing heartily comes from James Paulding: "Mr. Madison had undertaken to substitute Beer in the room of whiskey, as a beverage for his slaves in Harvest time, and on one occasion, I remember, stopt on a wheat field . . . to inquire how they liked the new drink—'O! vere fine—vere fine masser' said one old grey head—'but I tink a glass of whiskey very good to make it wholesome!' He was excessively diverted at this supplement of the old fellow, and often made merry with it afterwards" (619).

Much of Madison's time in his retirement was devoted to attempts to end slavery. He believed that a civilized, democratic society could gradually and fairly abolish this "deep-rooted and widespread evil" (625). By using money from the federal sale of Western lands, he reasoned that the government could purchase the slaves and free them. Because of "reciprocal antipathies" between African Americans and European Americans, Madison hoped the newly freed slaves would be given a new home in Africa, away from the scenes of their degradation, where they would be able to develop their human potential. He helped found the American Colonization Society with Henry Clay, Bushrod Washington, John Marshall, and others, to resettle freed slaves in Liberia. If, over twenty years, the national government appropriated $600 million from the sale (at two dollars an acre) of one-third of the new Western lands, Madison believed it would provide $400 to buy each of the one and a half million slaves in America and transport them to West Africa (626). Madison wrote Lafayette in 1820 of "the dreadful fruit" of the "original sin" of slavery, and he encouraged those who ridiculed his plan of gradual emancipation to give alternative ideas to end the moral tragedy that threatened to destroy the American republic and Union (627). As president of the American Colonization Society, he blamed the South's economic depression on the institution of slavery and praised instances of private manumission (628).

Concerning other social developments at this time, Madison deemed Robert Owen's utopian socialist experiment impractical given "the impossibility of banishing evil altogether from human society."[7] His Christian belief in original sin, the persistence of human selfishness and greed only redeemable through Christ and controlled by the Holy Spirit, left Madison skeptical of socialist or communal arrangements premised on "nice" human nature. At best they were deluded about the true nature of man; at worst they were a prideful refusal to acknowledge the evil in the human heart—an evil cured only by a humble acceptance of God's grace and love. All utopian schemes were a "panacea," ignorant of the true human condition of human wickedness and therefore dangerous. Owen's system relied upon the unbiblical assumptions that man's curse of labor could be "relished" and in, Madison's words, that "love of equality will supercede the [human] desire of distinction" and that increased leisure will lead to noble pursuits rather than "the vicious resorts for the ennui of idleness."[8] History and Scripture both contradict this optimistic assessment for the Calvinist Madison.

In 1829, at the age of 78, Madison was elected as a delegate from Orange County to the Virginia convention planning to write a new state constitution. This return to constitution-building seemed to invigorate the elder statesman. Another delegate found him "rejuvenated . . . his cheerfulness and amenity and abundant stock of racy anecdotes were the delight of every social board." James Monroe and John Marshall were also in attendance, but Madison was the sole surviving member of the 1776 Virginia Convention.[9]

Madison advocated changing the state constitution to extend voting rights to all householders who paid state taxes, not just landowners or "freeholders." Basing his argument on Lockean categories of government designed to protect "life, liberty, and property," Madison held that even citizens not possessing real property had "a sufficient stake in the public order and the stable administration of the laws" to qualify for participation in governance.[10] "Persons and property, are the objects on which government is to act: and the rights of persons, and the rights of property are the objects for the protection of which Government was instituted. These rights cannot be separated. The personal right to acquire property, which is a natural right, gives to property when acquired a right to protection as a social right."[11] Besides, with the rapid increase in population in the United States, Madison saw more Americans living in towns and cities, which did not have the farms and lands requisite to freeholder suffrage. Sounding a more classical republican note emphasizing the educative value of public participation, though, Madison argued that extending the "partnership of power" would foster that political and moral influence emanating from the actual possession of authority and bring about a just and beneficial exercise of it (393).

Both these rationales for extending voting rights and advocating constitutional reform were grounded in his Christian appreciation of the potential corrupting effects of allowing a minority to assume all power. "Man is known to be a selfish as well as a social being. Respect for character though often a salutary restraint, is but too often overruled by other [i.e. selfish] motives. . . . We all know that conscience is not a sufficient safeguard, besides that conscience itself may be deluded . . . [and] present temptation is too often found to be an over match for those considerations." Moral self-restraint in power, especially of the non-elect (i.e., non-Christian, whose consciences are not fortified by the Spirit of Christ) "can never be relied on as a guaranty of the rights of the minority against a majority disposed to take advantage of its power" (390). Hence, as he had in defense of the checks and balances of federalism and various branches in the national government, Madison insisted that in Virginia, "the only effectual safeguard to the rights of minorities must be laid in such a basis and structure of the Government itself" (390–91). During a particularly acrimonious conflict in this Virginia constitutional convention, Madison reminded the delegates of a similar impasse during the writing of the U.S. Constitution and attributed its resolve to "a miracle," adding that he could not "but flatter [him]self, that, without a miracle, we shall be able to arrange all difficulties" with a spirit of compromise (392).

Madison also engaged in controversies over the meaning and development of American federalism throughout his last years. As author of many *Federalist Papers* and esteemed "Father of the Constitution," he was drawn upon to support all positions, and advocates often quoted him on both sides of a constitutional issue. This proved embarrassing to him at times, especially given his advancing age and sensitivity to charges of "ruling from the grave" and displaying senility. But he could not forgo entering into political debates when he saw one or the other side (be it those arguing for excessive nationalism or extreme states' rights), and the human evil behind it, gaining a destructive ascendancy. Madison's states' rights emphasis emerged in reaction to Chief Justice John Marshall's indiscriminate expansion of federal power in various Supreme Court decisions. He insisted that Marshall's expansion of Congressional authority through reliance on the formal *means* used to perform constitutional ends was a threat to balanced federalism: "To give an extent to the . . . means [of government] superceding the limits of [its objects] is in effect to convert a limited into an unlimited Government." Still, he acknowledged that the Court's decision in *McCulloch v. Maryland* rightfully denied a state the power to tax a federal institution. In the *Cohens v. Virginia* ruling, however, Madison resented Marshall's "apparent disposition to amplify the authorities of the Union at the expense of those of the States." Chief Justice Marshall's "ingenious and fatal sophistries" threatened balanced federalism, he warned.[12] In the long run, Madison did concur with the court's final jurisdiction in federal matters, since granting that authority to the states would upset "the vital principle of equality, which cements their Union—thus gradually be deprived of its virtue."[13]

Since his days as a representative in the Continental Congress during the American Revolutionary War, Madison had held that the national government's prerogative in foreign affairs gave it authority over tariffs or impost taxes. When the nullification controversy arose during the 1820s the federal right to impose international tariffs arose again, some states asserting control over taxation of imports. Madison quickly reminded correspondents that the intention of the constitutional framers was to house regulation of international trade in Congress. "Such a use of the power by Congress accords with the intention and expectation of the States in transferring the power over trade from themselves to the Government of the U.S. This was emphatically the case in the Eastern, the more manufacturing members of the Confederacy." This conforms with every other nation's practice of facing foreign countries in a unified way, because "if Congress have not the power it is annihilated for the nation; a policy without example in any other nation."[14] Without such uniform national trade regulations "there would be an end to that stability in Government and in Laws which is essential to good Government and good Laws; a stability the want of which is the imputation which has at all times been leveled against Republicanism with most effect by its most dexterous adversaries."[15] Reminiscent of his *Federalist Papers* phase, during which he invoked higher powers as he called for national order and stability, Madison's appeal for uniform American tariffs included a reference to Providence. He wrote in 1828: "May it not be regarded as among the Providential blessings to these States, that their geographical relations multiplied as they will be by artificial channels of [commerce], give such additional force to the many obligations to cherish that Union which alone secures their peace, . . . safety, and . . . prosperity."[16]

Responding to the controversy over nullification—the doctrine of John C. Calhoun of South Carolina that individual states can nullify federal laws that they find unconstitutional—which ultimately grew into the Civil War, Madison concluded his political writings with two lengthy treatises on the nature of American federalism, refuting the nullification ideology. This was especially important, since he was being cited as a principal advocate of states' rights in his 1798–99 Virginia Resolutions. In an article in the *North American Review* in 1830 and in his extensive "Notes on Nullification" (1833–36), Madison literally ended his political and intellectual life with these issues. A brief epistle entitled "Advice to My Country," found after his death (and dated fall of 1834), reiterated his views on the sanctity of the federal Union.

In his *North American Review* piece, Madison argued that the central government established by the U.S. Constitution was formed by the people of the states and therefore possesses authority over individuals in those states equal to that of the state constitutions within its delegated sphere (foreign relations, coinage, interstate commerce, etc.). "Being thus derived from the same source as the Constitutions of the States, it has, within each State, the same authority as the Constitution of the State; and is as much a Constitution in the strict sense of the term within its prescribed sphere, as the Constitutions of the States are, within their respective spheres."[17] Madison stated that controversies arising over the jurisdiction of those spheres are first to be handled by the federal judiciary, as the U.S. Constitution grants it "to all cases in law and equity arising under the Constitution" (400).

The constitution gives states control over the national regime through the election of representatives to the central legislature and the power to impeach both federal executive and judicial personnel. But Madison insisted that "those who have denied or doubted the supremacy of the Judicial power of the United States and denounce at the same time a nullifying power in a State, seem not to have sufficiently averted to the utter inefficiency of a supremacy in a law of the Land, without a supremacy in the exposition and execution of the law; nor to the destruction of all equipoise between Federal Government and the State Governments," if no mechanism for coordinated policy existed in the central government (401). The proper state action against federal usurpation provided in the U.S. Constitution is amendment to the constitution, which the states can initiate. Only after all constitutional remedies are tried can a single state renounce the compact. Without such extreme circumstances, Madison finds the actions sanctioned by nullification theory "inadmissible" because, as had happened under the Articles of Confederation, "it puts the power of the smallest fraction" against the vast majority. His Virginia Resolutions, so often cited for support by the nullifiers, Madison insists contained "no reference whatever to a constitutional right in an individual state, to arrest by force the operation of a law of the United States" (402–3). Rather, they called for concerted action by the several states to abolish the federal usurpation in the Alien and Sedition Acts. This is confirmed, Madison noted, by their communication to every other state in an attempt to constitutionally end the usurpative federal acts.

Notes on Nullification

James Madison's last systematic testimony on American federalism came in a long treatise written over a two-year period (1835–36) in response to Calhoun's nullification theory. This final testament to Madisonian political thought dwells heavily upon the Virginia Resolutions and his Report on the Virginia Resolutions, because these earlier writings were most frequently cited by the nullifiers in support of their cause. Madison scrupulously denied this extrapolation of his writings against the Alien and Sedition Acts in 1798–99. But even within this narrower context of argument, Madison expounded his classical, balanced view of federalism as necessary to control the excess of either local or centralized tyranny fueled by sinful humans' natural tendency to want to dominate others.

Holding that the "doctrine of nullification," as promulgated by a committee of the House of Representatives of the state of South Carolina in 1828, asserted that "a single State has a constitutional right to arrest the execution of a law of the U.S.," Madison described it as a "deformity" of constitutional interpretation with a "forbidding aspect of a naked creed" of states' rights confederacy.[18] Madison declared the nullifiers' use of the Virginia Resolutions in support of their cause "a perverted construction" of his arguments in the Resolutions and the Report on the Virginia Resolutions (418). He explained that the real object of those Virginia writings was to "produce a conviction everywhere [in the nation], that the Constitution had been violated by the obnoxious [Alien and Sedition] Acts and to procure a concurrence and cooperation of the other States in effectuating a repeal of the acts" (419). This intent is so different from "this spurious doctrine of nullification" that Madison could not imagine "a more fatal inlet to anarchy" (420). That a *single* state in the Union could infer a right to nullify federal law from the Virginia Resolutions was "so novel, so anomalous and so anarchical" for Madison that it "was not and could not be anticipated" in Virginia in the 1790s. The chaos produced by each state determining which federal statutes it accepted would render nullification "as abortive in practice as it would be incongruous in theory." Madison writes that these "startling consequences" result from the "extravagant presumption," or pride, of its proponents (421).

This reflection on "the human character," along with the lessons in history of other countries and of America's own "defective Confederation," led Madison to regard the nullifiers' claims as "a deadly poison," causing a "defaced and demolished" country (422). The chief "fallacy of their claim" to be in the Virginia Resolutions tradition remained the nullifiers' insistence that a "solitary or separate interposition" is advanced by them (423). Regardless of whether or not a constitutional right for a single state to resist a usurpative federal law exists in the abstract, Madison insists that the South Carolina interpretation of the nullification doctrine provides "the absurdity of such a claim" in its most "naked and suicidal form" (427). It would be suicidal for the Union, the nation, and ultimately each state, producing "a scene of unexampled confusion and distraction" (428). Calhoun's "degenerate" version of the Virginia Resolutions and the report was simply, for Madison, "an apocryphal version of the text" (426–27). This comparison of South Carolina's "factitious gloss" to heretical religious doctrines based on false Scriptures reiterates Madison's belief in the purity of the American federalist creed and the sinful evil of its willful perversion. In Calvinist fashion, he ascribed it to "that anomalous conceit" that sinful human nature is prone towards. The final rebuttal of the nullifiers' invocation of a Virginia state precedent for their heresies is Madison's reference to the Resolutions' "invitation" to other states to join them in their protests, revealing a recognition of the power of several states to constitutionally overturn a criminal federal act (433).

The proper remedy for centralized tyranny in America or in any government "established and organized on free principles" is, first, "the checks provided among the constituted authorities"; second, "the influence of the Ballot-boxes and Hustings"; and finally, the constitutional powers to "amend or remake it" (434). If none of these constitutional means satisfy a single state within the Union, Madison implies, that state must accept the legal decisions of the majority of the country. Sovereignty in America residing "not in a single state but in the people of each of the several states . . . the people of the several states must be a sovereign as they are a united people" (437). The "obvious fallacy" of Calhoun is, to Madison, a "painful . . . sophism" (436). "In conclusion, those who deny the possibility of a political system, with a divided sovereignty like that of the U.S. must choose between a government purely consolidated, and an association of Governments purely federal" (440).

Finally, in his posthumously published "Advice to My Country" (October 1834), Madison, in classically Christian language, warned of the danger of disunion: "The advice nearest to my heart and deepest in my convictions is that the Union of the States be cherished and perpetuated. Let the open enemy to it be regarded as a Pandora with her box opened; and the disguised one, as the Serpent creeping with his deadly wiles into Paradise."[19]

So, James Madison's political philosophy ended much as it had begun sixty years earlier during the American Revolution and construction of the U.S. Constitution, with an emphasis on federalism balancing centralized and decentralized governments, Lockean and classical ideologies moderating the potential excesses of either, grounded in a Christian view of human nature and society.

APPENDIX A

EXTRACT FROM
"THE REPORT ON THE
[VIRGINIA] RESOLUTIONS"

House of Delegates, Session of 1799–1800

Report of the Committee to Whom Were Referred
the Communications of Various States, Relative to
the Resolutions of the Last General Assembly of
this State, Concerning the Alien and Sedition Laws

Whatever room might be found in the proceedings of some of the states, who have disapproved of the resolutions of the General Assembly of this commonwealth, passed on the 21st day of December, 1798, for painful remarks on the spirit and manner of those proceedings, it appears to the committee most consistent with the duty, as well as dignity, of the General Assembly, to hasten an oblivion of every circumstance which might be construed into a diminution of mutual respect, confidence, and affection, among the members of the Union.

The committee have deemed it a more useful task to revise, with a critical eye, the resolutions which have met with their disapprobation; to examine fully the several objections and arguments which have appeared against them; and to inquire whether there can be any errors of fact, of principle, or of reasoning, which the candor of the General Assembly ought to acknowledge and correct.

The *first* of the resolutions is in the words following:

Resolved, That the General Assembly of Virginia doth unequivocally express a firm resolution to maintain and defend the Constitution of the United States, and the Constitution of this state, against every aggression, either foreign or domestic; and that they will support the government of the United States in all measures warranted by the former.

No unfavorable comment can have been made on the sentiments here expressed. To maintain and defend the Constitution of the United States, and of their own state, against every aggression, both foreign and domestic, and to support the government of the United States in all measures warranted by their Constitution, are duties which the General Assembly ought always to feel, and to which, on such an occasion, it was evidently proper to express their sincere and firm adherence.

In their *next* resolution—

The General Assembly most solemnly declares a warm attachment to the union of the states, to maintain which it pledges all its powers; and that, for this end, it is their duty to watch over and oppose every infraction of those principles which constitute the only basis of the Union, because a faithful observance of them can alone secure its existence and the public happiness.

The observation just made is equally applicable to this solemn declaration of warm attachment to the Union, and this solemn pledge to maintain it; nor can any question arise among enlightened friends of the Union, as to the duty of watching over and opposing every infraction of those principles which constitute its basis, and a faithful observance of which can alone secure its existence, and the public happiness hereon depending.

The *third* resolution is in the words following:

That this Assembly doth explicitly and peremptorily declare, that it views the powers of the federal government as resulting from the compact to which the states are parties, as limited by the plain sense and intention of the instrument constituting the compact—as no further valid than they are authorized by the grants enumerated in that compact; and that, in case of a deliberate, palpable, and dangerous exercise of other powers, not granted by the said compact, the states who are parties thereto have the right, and are in duty bound, to interpose, for arresting the progress of the evil, and for maintaining, within their respective limits, the authorities, rights, and liberties appertaining to them.

On this resolution the committee have bestowed all the attention which its importance merits. They have *scanned* it not merely with a strict, but with a severe eye; and they feel confidence in pronouncing that, in its just and fair construction, it is unexceptionably true in its several positions, as well as constitutional and conclusive in its inferences.

LAST TESTAMENT

"Advice to My Country"

As THIS ADVICE, if it ever see the light will not do it till I am no more, it may be considered as issuing from the tomb, where truth alone can be respected, and the happiness of man alone consulted. It will be entitled therefore to whatever weight can be derived from good intentions and from the experience of one who has served his country in various stations through a period of forty years, who espoused in his youth and adhered through his life to the cause of its liberty, and who has borne a part in most of the great transactions which will constitute epochs of its destiny.

The advice nearest to my heart and deepest in my convictions is the Union of the States be cherished and perpetuated. Let the open enemy to it be regarded as a Pandora with her box opened; and the disguised one, as the Serpent creeping with his deadly wiles into Paradise.

NOTES

INTRODUCTION

1. See, for example, Paul Rahe, *Republics Ancient and Modern* (Chapel Hill: University North Carolina Press, 1992); Michael P. Zuckert, *Natural Rights and the New Republicanism* (Princeton: Princeton University Press, 1994), and *The Natural Rights Republic* (Notre Dame, Ind.: University of Notre Dame Press, 1996); Gordon Wood, *The Creation of the American Republic* (Chapel Hill: University of North Carolina Press, 1969); J. G. A. Pocock, *The Machiavellian Moment* (Princeton: Princeton University Press, 1969); Bernard Bailyn, *The Ideological Origins of the American Revolution* (Cambridge: Harvard University Press, 1967); Donald Lutz, *A Preface to American Political Theory* (Lawrence, Kans.: University Press of Kansas, 1992); Lance Banning, *The Sacred Fire of Liberty: James Madison and the Founding of the Federal Republic* (Ithaca: Cornell University Press, 1995), 10.

2. James Madison, Alexander Hamilton, and John Jay, *The Federalist Papers*, ed. Isaac Kramnick (New York: Penguin, 1987) #55, #37, #51, #40, #57, #10 and #16; see esp. 339, 124, 242, 245, 319, 266, 344–345. Pages listed for *Federalist Papers* refer to this Penguin edition. The Calvinist notion of human "depravity" distinguishes it from both Medieval Catholic and Arminian Protestant theology. See John Calvin, *Institutes of the Christian Religion*, ed. John McNeill (Philadelphia: Westminster Press, 1960), I.i.i; Kenneth Latourette, *A History of Christianity* (New York: Harper and Row, 1975), 2:754, 959.

3. *Book of Confessions* (Louisville, Ky.: Office of the General Assembly, 1996), 132.

4. *Federalist* #10, 104; #6, 124. Cf. Calvin, *Institutes*, I.i.i-ii.

5. Marvin Meyers, *The Mind of the Founder* (Hanover, N.H.: University Press of New England, 1981), 37.

6. *Book of Confessions*, 147.

7. Meyers, *The Mind of the Founder*, 443.

8. The best exception to this scholarly deficiency is Ralph Ketcham's excellent biography *James Madison* (Charlottesville: University Press of Virginia, 1990), which is sensitive throughout to the place of Madison's religious heritage in his life and thought.

9. James Madison to William Bradford, September 25, 1773, in *The Papers of James Madison,* ed. William T. Hutchinson and William M. E. Rachal (Chicago: University of Chicago Press, 1962), 1:96; "Memorial and Remonstrance against Religious Assessments," June 1785, and James Madison to Harvard President Edward Everett, March 19, 1823, in Merrill D. Peterson, ed., *James Madison: A Biography in His Own Words* (New York: Harper and Row, 1974), 92–94, 382.

10. This may also be seen as part of a recent growth of scholarship in early American political theory that is rediscovering the religious dimensions of many founders. See, for example, Mark Hall, *The Political and Legal Philosophy of James Wilson* (Columbia, Mo.: University of Missouri, 1997) and Daniel Dreisbach, *Religion and Politics in the Early Republic* (Lexington, Ky.: University of Kentucky Press, 1996).

11. James Madison to Jasper Adams, spring 1833, and James Madison to Frederick Beasley, November 20, 1825, in Robert S. Alley, *James Madison on Religious Liberty* (Buffalo, N.Y.: Prometheus, 1985), 87, 85.

12. See John M. Murrin, "Religion and Politics in America from the First Settlements to the Civil War" in Mark Noll, ed., *Religion and American Politics* (New York: Oxford University Press, 1990), 34.

13. One might wish to attribute Madison's skepticism toward human nature to Thomas Hobbes and his vision of avaricious creatures in the state of nature, but there is no evidence of a Hobbesian influence on Madison while the Calvinist Christian perspective was pervasive in early America. See James M. Hutson, ed., *Religion and the New Republic* (Lanham, Md.: Rowman and Littlefield, 2000) esp. ch. 5, "Evangelicals in the American Founding," 190; Lance Banning, *The Sacred Fire of Liberty* (Ithaca: Cornell University Press, 1995); James H. Smylie, "Madison and Witherspoon: Theological Roots of American Political Thought," *Princeton University Library Chronicle* 22 (spring 1961); Irving Brant, *James Madison* (Indianapolis: Bobbs-Merrill, 1941), 119; Ketcham, *James Madison,* 46–48; Alley, *James Madison on Religious Liberty*; and Michael P. Zuckert, *The Natural Rights Republic* (Notre Dame, Ind.: University of Notre Dame Press, 1996). This evidence makes Lance Banning's statement that "religious topics simply disappear from his surviving writings after 1776" misleading (*The Sacred Fire of Liberty,* 80). It may be that some twentieth-century scholars project their own religious skepticism back onto eighteenth-century figures.

One: INTELLECTUAL HERITAGE

1. Lance Banning, *The Sacred Fire of Liberty* (Ithaca: Cornell University Press, 1995), 9.

2. Ralph Ketcham, *James Madison* (Charlottesville: University Press of Virginia, 1990), 19.

3. Merrill D. Peterson, ed., *James Madison: A Biography in His Own Words* (New York: Harper and Row, 1974), 44.

4. Mary-Elaine Swanson, *The Education of James Madison* (Montgomery, Ala.: Hoffman Center, 1992), 2.

5. Peterson, *James Madison*, 129.

6. Ketcham, *James Madison*, 259.

7. Swanson, *Education of James Madison*, 20, 21.

8. See Charles S. Sydnor, *Gentleman Freeholders* (Chapel Hill: University of North Carolina Press, 1952); Rhys Isaac, *The Transformation of Virginia* (Chapel Hill: University of North Carolina Press, 1982); Thomas Wertenbaker, *Patrician and Plebian in Virginia* (New York: Russell and Russell, 1959).

9. Peterson, *James Madison*, 14–15. See also Isaac, *Transformation of Virginia*.

10. James Madison, "Notes and Documents, James Madison's Autobiography," ed. Douglas Adair, *William and Mary Quarterly* 2 (April 1945): 195.

11. Swanson, *Education of James Madison*, 21–22, 24.

12. Ibid., 24.

13. Irving Brant, *James Madison* (Indianapolis: Bobbs-Merrill, 1941), 62.

14. Ibid., 24–25 and Ketcham, *James Madison*, 20–21.

15. *The Papers of James Madison*, ed. William T. Hutchinson and William M. E. Rachal (Chicago: University of Chicago Press, 1962), 1:13.

16. Ibid., 1:5 (Robertson's "Account Book," 11, 20, 65–66, 69, 72, 74, 78, 80–81, 132–37, 143).

17. Brant, *James Madison*, 58.

18. James Madison to Rev. Thomas Martin, August 10, 1769, in Swanson, *Education of James Madison*, 30.

19. Swanson, *Education of James Madison*, 24–26.

20. Brant, *James Madison*, 73, 77.

21. See Alan Heimert and Perry Miller, *The Great Awakening* (Indianapolis: Bobbs-Merrill, 1967).

22. Mark Noll, *Princeton and the Republic, 1768–1872* (Princeton: Princeton University Press, 1989), 17.

23. For example, see *Memoirs of Jonathan Edwards* in *The Works of Jonathan Edwards* (Peabody, Mass.: Hendrickson Publishers, 1998), lxxxiv–cxvii.

24. Noll, *Princeton and the Republic*, 8–9, 20, 21, 34.

25. In Robert S. Alley, ed., *James Madison on Religious Liberty* (Buffalo, N.Y.: Prometheus, 1985), 38, 43.

26. Peterson, *James Madison*, 18–22, 127.

27. Brant, *James Madison,* 84, 87.
28. Swanson, *Education of James Madison,* 101.
29. Ibid., 29.
30. Ibid., 107–9.
31. Hutchinson and Rachal, *Papers of James Madison,* vol. 1, "Commentary on the Bible, 1770–1773," 58. A few pages of Madison's Bible notes have been lost; the only remaining valid document containing the missing Bible excerpts is the biography written by William C. Rives, *History of the Life and Times of James Madison,* 3 vols. (Boston: Little, Brown, and Co., 1850–68). See, generally, Anita Rivera Simpkins, "James Madison on Education," Ph.D. diss., University of Virginia, Department of Education, May 1998.
32. For background on these, see Bernard Bailyn, *The Ideological Origins of the American Revolution* (Cambridge: Harvard University Press, 1967) and J. G. A. Pocock, *The Machiavillian Movement* (Princeton: Princeton University Press, 1969).
33. John Witherspoon, *Lectures on Moral Philosophy,* ed. Jack Scott (Newark, Del.: University of Delaware Press, 1982), 1 (hereafter *LMP*).
34. Ibid., 4. Brant describes Witherspoon's theological orientation as "orthodox and conservative" (*James Madison,* 77); Smylie describes it as "Presbyterian evangelical" (James H. Smylie, "Madison and Witherspoon: Theological Roots of American Political Thought," *Princeton University Library Chronicle* 22 [spring 1961]: 120); Noll terms it "evangelical" ("Evangelicals in the American Founding" in James Hutson, ed., *Religion and the New Republic* [Lanham, Md.: Rowman and Littlefield, 2000], 150). See also John West, *The Politics of Revelation and Reason* (Lawrence, Kans.: University Press of Kansas, 1996). Jeffrey Morrison captures Witherspoon's theological perspective best as "orthodox" Christianity, see Jeffrey Hays Morrison, "John Witherspoon and 'The Public Interest of Religion,'" *Journal of Church and State* 41 (summer 1999).
35. John Witherspoon, "Dominion of Providence," quoted in Morrison, "John Witherspoon and 'The Public Interest of Religion'"; *LMP*, 4.
36. Noll, *Princeton and the Republic,* 24.
37. *LMP,* 8.
38. Brant, *James Madison,* 77; Hutchinson and Rachal, *Papers of James Madison,* 1:83.
39. Smylie, "Madison and Witherspoon," 124.
40. Ketcham, *James Madison,* 35, 231, 43–44, 46–48.
41. Swanson, *Education of James Madison,* 54.
42. In the words of Professor Smylie, "The imprint of Witherspoon is clearly evident" ("Madison and Witherspoon," 124).

43. Witherspoon, "Lectures on Divinity," in Smylie, "Madison and Witherspoon," 121.

44. Smylie, "Madison and Witherspoon," 121.

45. Witherspoon, "Part of a Speech in Congress, upon the Confederation," in *The Works of John Witherspoon*, 9 vols. (Edinburgh: Ogle and Aikman, 1804–5), 4:350, quoted in Smylie, "Madison and Witherspoon," 123.

46. Quoted in Smylie, "Madison and Witherspoon," 128.

47. James Madison, *Federalist #51*, in James Madison, Alexander Hamilton, and John Jay, *The Federalist Papers*, ed. Isaac Kramnick (New York: Penguin 1987), 319. Pages listed for *Federalist Papers* refer to this Penguin edition. See also *Federalist #48*, 311: "the powers of government should be so divided and balanced among several bodies of magistracy as that no one could transcend their legal limits without being effectually checked and restrained by the others."

48. Witherspoon, *Works* 3:435 and 4:351, 349, quoted in Smylie, "Madison and Witherspoon," 123, 124.

49. Kramnick, ed., *Federalist Papers*, 124, 127.

50. Smylie, "Madison and Witherspoon," 124, 132.

51. Ashbel Green, "The Life of the Revd John Witherspoon," Manuscript in New Jersey Historical Society archive; microfilm in Princeton University Library. Quoted in Smylie, "Madison and Witherspoon," 130. Professor Smylie concludes: "Without preaching a sermon and yet relying upon his theological orientation, Madison translated the views of Witherspoon and the nature of man into a political instrument" (131).

52. *LMP*, 140, cf. John Locke, *Second Treatise on Government*, ed. Peter Laslett (New York: New American Library, 1965), 95.

53. *LMP*, 141, cf. Locke, *Second Treatise*, ch. 15, 171.

54. *LMP*, 123, cf. Locke, *Second Treatise*, ch. 8, 99.

55. Cf. Aristotle, *The Politics*, ed. T. A. Sinclair (New York: Penguin, 1972), 209–11.

56. Cf. ibid., 225–27.

57. Cf. ibid., 207.

58. "This corruption of nature, during this life, does remain in those that are regenerated." Westminster Confession 6:v; *Book of Confessions* (Louisville, Ky.: Office of the General Assembly, 1996), 132.

59. This is a direct reference to the Westminster Confession, 23:iii, *Book of Confessions*, 151.

60. *Book of Confessions*, 138.

61. C. S. Lewis, *Mere Christianity*, bk.2, ch. 3. Cf. the Westminster Confession, 6:i. and John Calvin, *Institutes of the Christian Religion*, ed. John Mc-

Neill (Philadelphia: Westminster Press, 1960), I.1.i. As twentieth-century Oxford apologist C. S. Lewis summarizes it:

> The moment you have a self at all, there is a possibility of putting yourself first—wanting to be the center—wanting to be God, in fact. That was the sin of Satan: and that was the sin he taught the human race. . . . What Satan put into the heads of our remote ancestors was the idea that they could "be like Gods"—could set up on their own as if they had created themselves—be their own masters—invent some sort of happiness for themselves outside God, apart from God. And out of that hopeless attempt has come nearly all that we call human history—money, poverty, ambition, war, prostitution, classes, empires, slavery—the long terrible story of man trying to find something other than God which will make him happy.

62. St. Augustine, *Political Writings,* ed. H. Paolucci (Chicago: Regnery, 1962), 1–2.

63. Ketcham, *James Madison,* 652–53.

64. Calvin, *Institutes,* 2:243.

65. Ibid., 2:290.

66. Ibid., 2:291, 2:247, 2:48.

67. *LMP,* 66.

68. Noll, *Princeton and the Republic,* 24.

69. Peterson, *James Madison,* 23. Similarly, Madison employs a Calvinist predestination argument in a letter to Samuel Stanhope Smith; see Ketcham, *James Madison,* 83–84.

70. Peterson, *James Madison,* 23, 24.

71. *Federalist* #55, 339; #5, 124; #10, 165; #19; #10, 124.

72. *Federalist* #85, 484; #6, 104.

73. Peterson, *James Madison,* 23–24, 103–6, 87, 42. Madison even argued for the classic Calvinist predestination view in a letter to his Princeton classmate Samuel Stanhope Smith (84).

74. Ibid., 57, 74; Ketcham, *James Madison,* 65.

75. James Madison to Thomas Jefferson, October 17, 1788, and "Debates in the Federal Convention," both in Peterson, *James Madison,* 164, 134–35.

76. On other aspects of Madison's Christian orthodoxy, see Brant, *James Madison,* 119; Ketcham, *James Madison,* 46–48; and Smylie, "Madison and Witherspoon," 119.

77. James Madison to William Bradford, July 1, 1774, in Hutchinson and Rachal, *Papers of James Madison,* 1:114.

78. James Madison to William Bradford, December 1, 1773, in Hutchinson and Rachal, *Papers of James Madison,* 1:101, 26, and Ketcham, *James Madison,* 51–60.

Two: POLITICS AND RELIGION

1. Gaillard Hunt, *Life of James Madison* (New York: Russell and Russell, 1902), 4. Ralph Ketcham, *James Madison* (Charlottesville: University Press of Virginia, 1990), 58. This state religion was contrary to the English Calvinist Westminster Confession (23: iii): "it is the duty of civil magistrates to protect the Church of our common Lord, without giving preference to any denominations of Christians above the rest." *Book of Confessions* (Louisville, Ky.: Office of the General Assembly, 1996), 151.

2. See Eusebius, *The History of the Church,* trans. G. A. Williamson (New York: Dorset, 1965), bk. 4.

3. Quoted in Jeffery Hays Morrison, "John Witherspoon and 'The Public Interest of Religion,'" *Journal of Church and State* 41 (summer 1999), 567.

4. James Madison to William Bradford, December 1, 1773, in Merrill D. Peterson, ed., *James Madison: A Biography in His Own Words* (New York: Harper and Row, 1974), 26.

5. Ketcham, *James Madison,* 72.

6. Peterson, *James Madison,* 91.

7. Ketcham, *James Madison,* 166.

8. Peterson, *James Madison,* 94.

9. Ketcham, *James Madison,* 167.

10. Quoted in Daniel L. Dreisbach, *Religion and Politics in the Early Republic* (Lexington, Ky.: University of Kentucky Press, 1996), 117.

11. Gordon Wood, *The Radicalism of the American Revolution* (New York: Random House, 1991), esp. 329–33.

Three: FEDERALIST NATIONALISM

1. Ralph Ketcham, *James Madison* (Charlottesville: University Press of Virginia, 1990), 142.

2. Merrill D. Peterson, ed., *James Madison: A Biography in His Own Words* (New York: Harper and Row, 1974), 47.

3. Ibid., 48, 49.

4. Ketcham, *James Madison,* 90.

5. Peterson, *James Madison,* 48.

6. Ibid., 49–50.

7. Ketcham, *James Madison,* 91.

8. Peterson, *James Madison,* 57.

9. Ibid., 47.

10. Ketcham *James Madison,* 95.

11. Ibid., 96

12. Ibid.

13. Peterson, *James Madison*, 101.
14. Ketcham, *James Madison*, 93.
15. Ibid., 94.
16. Ibid., 93, 122–23.
17. Peterson, *James Madison*, 64, 69.
18. Ketcham, *James Madison*, 123.
19. Ibid., 131.
20. Ibid., 113, 114.
21. Ibid., 114, 115.
22. Peterson, *James Madison*, 71–72.
23. Ketcham, *James Madison*, 185.
24. James Madison to Edmund Pendleton, Feb. 24, 1787, in Peterson, *James Madison*, 102.
25. Ketcham, *James Madison*, 183–84.
26. Peterson, *James Madison*, 103–6.

Four: LOCKEAN LIBERALISM REALIZED

1. James Madison, Alexander Hamilton, and John Jay, *The Federalist Papers*, ed. Isaac Kramnick (New York: Penguin, 1987), #85, 484; #40, 266; #37, 242. Pages listed for the *Federalist Papers* refer to this Penguin edition.
2. Ralph Ketcham, *James Madison* (Charlottesville: University Press of Virginia, 1990), 190; Merrill D. Peterson, ed., *James Madison: A Biography in His Own Words* (New York: Harper and Row, 1974), 130–31.
3. Peterson, *James Madison*, 131.
4. *Federalist* #51, 319.
5. Peterson, *James Madison*, 135.
6. See Garrett Ward Sheldon, *The Political Philosophy of Thomas Jefferson* (Baltimore: Johns Hopkins University Press 1991), ch. 4.
7. Peterson, *James Madison*, 147.
8. Ibid., 148–49.
9. Ketcham, *James Madison*, 197.
10. Peterson, *James Madison*, 144.
11. Ketcham, *James Madison*, 230.
12. Peterson, *James Madison*, 144.
13. Ketcham, *James Madison*, 231.
14. *Federalist* #10, 122.
15. See Garrett Ward Sheldon, *Religion and Politics* (New York: Peter Lang, 1990), 96, 99.
16. See Garrett Ward Sheldon, *The Political Philosophy of Thomas Jefferson* (Baltimore: Johns Hopkins University Press, 1991), 85–87.

17. See Garrett Ward Sheldon, *The History of Political Theory* (New York: Peter Lang, 1988), ch. 2.

18. *Federalist* #63, 373.

19. Ketcham, *James Madison,* 252, 251, 253.

20. Peterson, *James Madison,* 157.

21. Ketcham, *James Madison,* 258.

22. Ibid., 253.

Five: CLASSICAL REPUBLICANISM

1. Ralph Ketcham, *James Madison* (Charlottesville: University Press of Virginia, 1990), 391–92.

2. Ibid., 392; James Madison to Thomas Jefferson, May 12, 1791; May 20, 1798; and March 2, 1794, in Merrill D. Peterson, ed., *James Madison: A Biography in His Own Words* (New York: Harper and Row, 1974), 183, 222, 200.

3. See J. G. A. Pocock, *The Machiavellian Moment* (Princeton: Princeton University Press, 1969). For a lengthy discussion of the scholarly literature emerging from this paradigm, see my *The Political Philosophy of Thomas Jefferson* (Baltimore: Johns Hopkins University Press, 1991), 5–18, 148–70.

4. See Bernard Bailyn, *The Ideological Origins of the American Revolution* (Cambridge: Harvard University Press, 1967); Gordon Wood, *The Creation of the American Republic* (Chapel Hill: Union North Carolina Press, 1969).

5. See Paul Rahe, *Republics Ancient and Modern* (Chapel Hill: University North Carolina Press, 1992), 559; and Michael P. Zuckert, *The Natural Rights Republic* (Notre Dame: University of Notre Dame Press, 1996), 202–43.

6. Zuckert, *Natural Rights Republic,* 212, 243.

7. Peterson, *James Madison,* 178–82.

8. Ibid., 184–87.

9. Ibid., 192.

10. James Madison to Thomas Jefferson, Dec. 19, 1796, ibid., 210.

11. James Madison to Thomas Jefferson, May 20, 1798, ibid., 221.

12. From Gaillard Hunt, ed., *The Writings of James Madison* (New York: Putnams, 1906), 4:393–94.

13. Ketcham, *James Madison,* 393.

14. Hunt, *Writings of James Madison,* 6:326.

15. James Madison to Thomas Jefferson, Dec. 29, 1798, draws a distinction between "state" and "legislature" in who may nullify unconstitutional Federal acts. "On the supposition that the former [states] is clearly the ultimate Judge of infractions, it does not follow that the latter [state legislature] is the legitimate organ especially as a Convention was the organ by which the compact was made." Madison recommends the more general term "state" to

"leave to other states a choice of all the modes possible of concurring in the substance." Ibid., 6:328–29.

16. Ketcham, *James Madison*, 403.

17. Hunt, *Writings of James Madison*, 6:348.

Six: NATIONALISM REVISITED

1. Merrill D. Peterson, ed., *James Madison: A Biography in His Own Words* (New York: Harper and Row, 1974), 235; Ralph Ketcham, *James Madison* (Charlottesville: University Press of Virginia, 1990), 410.

2. Ketcham, *James Madison*, 410.

3. Ibid., 421.

4. James Madison to Robert Livingston, May 1, 1802, in Peterson, *James Madison*, 240.

5. James Madison to Charles Pinckney, May 11, 1802, in Peterson, *James Madison*, 241.

6. Peterson, *James Madison*, 245.

7. Garrett Ward Sheldon, *The Political Philosophy of Thomas Jefferson* (Baltimore: Johns Hopkins University Press, 1991), 96.

8. Ketcham, *James Madison*, 422.

9. Ibid., 456.

10. Sheldon, *The Political Philosophy of Thomas Jefferson*, 100.

11. Ketcham, *James Madison*, 457.

12. Sheldon, *The Political Philosophy of Thomas Jefferson*, 100.

13. Ketcham, *James Madison*, 418, 431.

14. Sheldon, *The Political Philosophy of Thomas Jefferson*, 100–101.

15. Ketcham, *James Madison*, 460.

16. Peterson, *James Madison*, 260.

17. Ketcham, *James Madison*, 460.

18. Ibid., 465, 466. Peterson, *James Madison*, 272.

19. Ketcham, *James Madison*, 492.

20. Quoted in Peterson, *James Madison*, 288.

21. Ketcham, *James Madison*, 501.

22. Ibid., 537, 538.

23. Swanson, *Education of James Madison*, 263.

24. Ibid., 263–64.

25. Ibid., 265.

26. Ketcham, *James Madison*, 491.

27. *Papers of James Madison*, Presidential Series, ed. J. C. A. Stagg (Charlottesville: University Press of Virginia, 1996), 3:137–38.

28. Peterson, *James Madison*, 357.

29. Ketcham, *James Madison,* 609.
30. Marvin Meyers, ed. *The Mind of the Founder* (Hanover, N.H.: University Press of New England, 1981), 390.
31. Peterson, *James Madison,* 363.

Seven: LAST TESTAMENTS

1. Ralph Ketcham, *James Madison* (Charlottesville: University Press of Virginia, 1990), 616.
2. Ibid., 630.
3. Marvin Meyers, ed. *The Mind of the Founder* (Hanover, N.H.: University Press of New England, 1981), 389.
4. Ketcham, *James Madison,* 630.
5. Merrill D. Peterson, ed., *James Madison: A Biography in His Own Words* (New York: Harper and Row, 1974), 367.
6. Ketcham, *James Madison,* 620.
7. James Madison to Thomas Jefferson, April 1827, in Peterson, *James Madison,* 388.
8. Ibid., 387–88.
9. Ketcham, *James Madison,* 636, 637.
10. Ketcham, *James Madison,* 637–38.
11. Peterson *James Madison,* 390.
12. Ketcham, *James Madison,* 632.
13. Ibid., 633.
14. Meyers, *The Mind of the Founder,* 372, 373.
15. Ketcham, *James Madison,* 636.
16. Meyers, *The Mind of the Founder,* 379.
17. Peterson, *James Madison,* 399.
18. Meyers, *The Mind of the Founder,* 418.
19. Peterson, *James Madison,* 407.

INDEX